TAO CONSCIOUSNESS

道符道

Tao-Chih-Tao
the process of becoming Tao is Tao

Future Books by Greg Leveille in This Series:

Tao Meditation Guide

Wu Wei Practice

The 22 Levels of Tao Consciousness

The Tao of Lao Tzu

The Tao of Ramana

The Tao of Sufi Mystics

The Tao of Sant Mat Mystics

TAO CONSCIOUSNESS

Before the Tao Te Ching and After Ramana

GREG LEVEILLE

Copyright © 2023 by Greg Leveille. All rights reserved.

Waterside Productions
2055 Oxford Ave.
Cardiff by the Sea, CA. 92007
www.waterside.com

All right reserved. No part of this book may be reproduced in any form or by any means, electronic or mechanical, including photocopying, recording, or by any information storage and retrieval system, without permission in writing from the publisher.

First Edition
Printed in the United States of America

This edition is printed on acid-free paper that meets the American National Standards Institute Z39.48 Standard.
This book is printed on 30% postconsumer recycled paper.
For more information, please visit **www.waterside.com**

Distributed by Waterside Productions, Inc.

Library of Congress Cataloging-in-Publication Data
Name: Leveille, Greg, 1948- Author
Title: Tao Consciousness before the Tao Te Ching and after Ramana
Description: First edition | Cardiff by the Sea, California: Waterside, 2023

Identifiers: ISBN-13: 978-1-958848-78-4 print edition
ISBN-13: 978-1-958848-79-1 e-book edition

CONTENTS

PUBLISHER'S NOTE	xi
PREFACE	xiii
Readers Notes	xv

CHAPTER 1

THE AGE OF TRIBES	1
The Spring Winds Were Late	2
Yu, the Greatest Shaman in the Land	3
Yu's Legend Grew	6
The Magical Steps of the Celestial Ladder	8
The Year of the Great Floods	9
The Dragon Gate	11

CHAPTER 2

THE AGE OF MYSTICS	15
The Evolution of Ancient Wisdom	16
The Enduring Legend of the Yellow Dragon	18
Tribal Shamans	19
The Creation Myths of Shamans	19
The Evolution of Great Saints	20
The Origin of Ancient, Mystic Taoism	23
The Taoist Heaven and Earth Jade Tablet	24
The Original Wu Wei Taoist Teaching	25
The Taoist Version of the Yellow Dragon	25
The Taoist Version of the Way to Heaven	26
The Taoist Version of the Celestial Net	28
The Path of the Yellow Dragon	29

CHAPTER 3

THE AGE OF EMPERORS — 31

- The Dawning of Chinese Civilization — 32
- Guang Chengzi and the Yellow Emperor — 34
- The Origin of Ancient, Mystic Taoism — 35
- Taoist Teachings during the Shang Dynasty — 37
- Development of the Chinese Language — 39
- Ancient Chinese Pictograms — 40
- Circles versus Squares and Lines — 41
- The Forgotten Ancient Taoist Tablets — 42
- Worldwide Power Struggles — 43
- The Chinese Mandate of Heaven — 43
- The Legalist Philosophy — 46
- Shang Yang and Han Feize — 46
- Conflicts with the Legalist Philosophy — 46
- The Legalist Impact on the Tao Te Ching — 47

CHAPTER 4

THE AGE OF ENLIGHTENMENT — 49

- Key Spiritual Events in Ancient China — 51
- Shaman Influence on Chinese Culture — 52
- Shaman Yarrow Sticks — 52
- The Shaman I-Ching — 54
- The Taoist Doctrine — 55
- The Foundational Tao Scriptures — 56
- Huang Long – 5000–50 BCE — 57
- Tai Shang Gan Ying Pian - 600 BCE — 57
- The Zuangzi – 450 BCE — 58
- The Nei-Yeh – 350 BCE — 58
- The Tao Te Ching – 250 BCE — 59
- The Popularity of Tao consciousness — 60
- Ancient Experiences in Tao Consciousness — 61
- Reincarnation — 62
- Taoist Immortals — 63
- From Mysticism to Religion — 65

CHAPTER 5

MEMOIRS OF A TAOIST SAGE — 67
- Wu Wei — All the Way — 69
- My First Discovery of Taoist Tablets — 77
- Hundreds of Ancient Tablets — 78
- Other Incredible Miracles — 81
- My Near-Death Experience — 81
- The Programmers Test at General Motors — 87
- The Speech at the Radha Soami Meeting — 88
- The Invention of the Spreadsheet — 88
- One Last Thing — 91

CHAPTER 6

THE AGE OF MODERN TAOISM — 95
- Tao Consciousness — 95
- Scholars versus Mystics — 98
- How Scholars Treat Mystical Writings — 98
- The Jade Sages of Ancient Taoism — 100
- The Vital Essence — 104
- How Does a Mystic Describe Tao? — 106
- The Heavenly Regions of Tao Consciousness — 108
- The Creative "Big Bang" Power of Tao — 110
- Tao Is Neither Water nor Breath — 113
- Following Breath toward Clear Awareness — 116
- Third-Eye Enlightenment — 118
- As the Crown Chakra Opens — 121
- Tao, Qi, Tian, and Zhohua — 123

CHAPTER 7

WHAT IS TAO CONSCIOUSNESS? — 127
- What Is Spiritual Enlightenment? — 128
- Choosing Some Easy Definitions — 130
  1. Spiritually Driven — 130
  2. Spiritually Minded — 131
  3. Spiritually Enlightened — 132

    4. Divinely Enlightened   132
    Twenty-Two Levels of Spiritual Enlightenment   133

CHAPTER 8

TAO-CHIH-TAO POEMS   135
- Tao Cosmology   136
  - Celestial Awareness   138
  - The Everlasting Instant   140
  - Heaven and Earth   142
  - Singularity and Polarity   143
  - Tao Is Within Yin and Yang   145
  - Tao Wind and Clouds   146
  - Heavenly Tao Creates Human Tao   148
- Tao Becomes Four States   149
  - Flowing To and From Tao   150
  - Tao Rises Like the Valley Mist   151
  - The Illusionary World   152
  - The Ocean and the Drop   154
- Who Were the Yellow Dragons?   155
  - The Huang Long Creates New Souls   157
  - Activation of the Vital Essence   159
  - Celestial Yellow Dragons   161
  - The Yellow Dragon Is Within You   162
- Three Types of Souls   163
  - Three Kinds of Souls in the Womb   164
  - Worldly Souls   166
  - The Celestial Net Traps the Mind   168
  - Getting Lost in Karma   171
  - Fragmented Awareness   172
  - Lost in Personal Perspective   173
  - Marked Souls   174
  - Sensing the Clouds and the Winds   176
  - Flying Through the Celestial Net   177
  - Jade Sage Souls   179
  - Within Wu-Chi Awareness   180

The Magical Life of Taoist Monks	181
The 3rd Soul Becomes a Jade Sage	182
Levels of Tao Enlightenment	183
3 Levels of Tao Enlightenment	184
Jade Sage Is a Yellow Dragon	186
The Jade Sage Is Magical	188
The Three Dragon Gates	190
The Tao-Chih-Tao Mantra	191
The Single-Word "Tao" Mantra	192
Practicing Celestial Tao Consciousness	195
Tao Is the Middle Way	196
The Differentiated Void	198
There Is Only One Soul, One Tao Consciousness	199
Ching, Ch'I, and Sheng	201
As the Middle Way Opens	202
Start Abiding in Equipoise	203
Abiding Inward and Outward	205
Tao Is Your Inner and Outer Guru	207
Abide in Joy, Wisdom, and Multiplicity	209
The Path Becomes Easier to Follow	211
Tao Consciousness Becomes Everything	213
Living within the Magical Middle Way	214
Becoming the Everlasting Instant	215

CHAPTER 9

THE TAO OF RAMANA	217
The Three Major Levels of Consciousness	218
The Basic Quest	218
Go Within — Beyond the Mind	219
Going Beyond the Knot of Karma	220
Mantra Repetition Helps New Seekers	221

CHAPTER 10

THE GOLDEN AGE OF TAO	223
A Time of Chaos	223
The Golden Age Has Begun	225

My Area of Focus	226
For more information on Tao:	228

ACKNOWLEDGMENTS 229

ABOUT THE AUTHOR 231

PUBLISHER'S NOTE

As a publisher and literary agent, I have overseen the publication of more than ten thousand titles that have sold hundreds of millions of copies and generated billions of dollars in book sales. I was conceived in 1949 according to my parents in part to manage my father's book publishing company ARCO PUBLISHING.

However, life is what happens when you are busy making other plans. Twenty-eight years later my father sold his publishing company and I moved to San Diego, where still in my twenties, I was given the opportunity to serve as editorial director for two different imprints at Harcourt Brace Jovanovich Publishing, one of the largest and most important publishing enterprises in America at that time.

I left two years later to create Waterside Productions as a film company and eventually literary agency, online education company, and publishing company.

Throughout these wonderful experiences I have been honored to publish or agent many great books including titles from Eckhart Tolle, Marie Kondo, Dr. and Master Zhi Gang Sha, Neale Donald Walsch, and major celebrities and visionary business leaders.

Of all these experiences, however, none matches the enthusiasm and sense of sacred responsibility I feel in serving as co-publisher with my wife, Gayle, for TAO CONSCIOUSNESS by author Greg Leveille.

Greg is not famous. He does not have millions or even tens of thousands of devoted followers. However, the book that you are about to read contains the highest level of wisdom of any book I have ever published, agented, or read.

In recent years I have become an expert on the Dao De Jing attributed to Lao Zhu over 2,500 years ago. As magnificent and powerful as the Dao De Jing is, the book you are holding in your hands or reading on your computer, TAO CONSCIOUSNESS, is even more profound.

Ten years ago, I would not have had the knowledge or awareness to fully appreciate the information shared by Greg. Most likely I would have been highly skeptical of the personal story Greg shares of how he came to write this book and the unusual journey he has taken as a human being.

On one level Greg is a very ordinary person living a very ordinary life. However, Greg is also perhaps the most unusual human being living on planet Earth at this time.

His insights and wisdom touch the core of the deepest questions each of us ever ask—who are we, where do we come from, where are we going, what is the purpose of our lives, what is the purpose of the universe, how was the universe created, and how do we co-exist in timeless eternities and retain our human qualities?

These and other questions will be answered for you if read and contemplate this book.

Enjoy the journey and realize that each of us, like Greg, has access to infinite potential and infinite grace.

With humility and gratitude for a life that has allowed me to present TAO CONSCIOUSNESS to the world…

William Gladstone

PREFACE

The history of ancient China is a fascinating tale of curious facts and mythological fiction. It's a legend about the earliest Chinese settlements, their shamans, and their cherished Creation beliefs. It's a story about powerful emperors, fabled dynasties, magical yellow dragons, heavenly deities, common people, and the Way of Heaven.

This is also the story about the true origins of mystical Taoism, and how it almost disappeared as it was slowly transformed into various new shamanistic, philosophical, and religious organizations – groups that also called themselves Taoist.

This book will also help you to understand the differences between tribal shaman trances, intellectual Chinese philosophy, legalist doctrine, and the celestial consciousness path of the original Taoist mystics.

The history of the ancient wisdom began on Earth seven thousand years ago in China, with the Taoist Path of the Yellow Dragon.

This book describes the real story about the ancient Taoist Path of the Yellow Dragon that ultimately become known as the Taoist Path of Celestial Awareness. This original Taoist path evolved thousands of years before the creation of both the I-Ching and the Tao Te Ching. It's the story about how these ancient sages used jade tablets to teach new seekers about the Taoist path.

This photograph depicts one of the most important tablets that the ancient Taoist sages used to explain the Path of the Yellow Dragon and the original nature of Tao consciousness.

This is a five-thousand-year-old Taoist meditation tablet carved out of translucent jade. The empty circle in the middle of this tablet illustrates the heavenly Tao consciousness that exists within our clear awareness and within the cosmos itself. It was also used to describe how heavenly Tao consciousness creates the ten thousand things (everything that exists) in the cosmos.

The yellow dragon symbol carved on the surface of the tablet was meant to remind new monks that meditating on pure Tao consciousness would enable them to travel beyond both the ten thousand things and the secret "ways to heaven."

It was because of sacred Taoist tablets like this that the Taoist saints were often called *Yu Shih* — which means *jade sage* in Old Chinese. In the early days, this Taoist path was probably called *huang long*, the Path of the Yellow Dragon.

I will explain this entire doctrine and how to reach divine Tao consciousness in much greater detail later in this book.

This book is also a valuable guide for modern students who want to understand how to reach, explore, and abide in successive levels of clear, Celestial Awareness - far beyond mind-body awareness.

The jade sage Taoists were the very first teachers on Earth to describe and teach highly advanced, celestial, meditation practices that enable direct enlightenment into spiritual consciousness — beyond both mind-body and space-time awareness. The modern direct consciousness and direct awakening doctrines of Sri Ramana, Nisargadatta Maharaj, and also my own, are nearly identical to the meditation techniques of the ancient Taoist sages.

I have been practicing this same Taoist path to *Jade Pure* Tao consciousness for my entire life. After sixty years of an intensive wu wei (effortless actions) meditation-based lifestyle, and twenty–five years of teaching this path, I understand the big picture of essential meditation practices very well.

This book is, thus, also a rare chronicle of the memoirs of a modern Taoist sage/teacher, comparable to the similar experiences of ancient Taoist sages.

When you fully understand the historical events that occurred during the two–thousand–year–old growth and decline of mystic Taoism, your understanding of what ancient Taoism meant to different generations of shamans, mystics, peasants, philosophers, and rulers will, most likely, be forever changed.

Moreover, when you fully experience mystic Taoism yourself, your entire life could become forever changed.

Readers Notes

The primary purpose of this book is to describe the ancient Chinese mystic Taoist path and the resultant mystic teachings and meditation

practices that began more than five thousand years before Lao Tzu's "Tao Te Ching."

You will also learn how to practice these same meditation techniques– and what to expect when you reach heavenly enlightenment through Tao consciousness.

The secondary objective of this book is to describe the mysterious, and somewhat elusive history of both the growth and the decline of mystic Taoism.

The following is a summary of the chapters:

Chapter 1: The Age of Tribes provides a story about how the legendary Chinese tribal fables about creation, yellow dragons, and the ways to heaven were created by mystical shamans.

Chapter 2: The Age of Mystics explains how the original Taoist Path of the Yellow Dragon used the most common tribal legends to show how and why the Taoist masters could teach new monks how to awaken and abide in Celestial Awareness.

Chapter 3: <u>The Age of Empires</u> describes the growth of the Chinese civilization during the Hsi, Shang, and Zhou dynasties and how it affected the acceptance and the growth of the original Taoist path.

Chapter 4: <u>The Age of Enlightenment</u> analyzes the impact that the path of Tao consciousness had on the emerging philosophies and religions during the Warring States period of the Zhou dynasty.

Chapter 5: <u>Memoirs of a Taoist Sage</u> describes my personal journey as a Taoist mystic and the types of miracles that occur as you journey into the higher regions of *Jade Pure* Tao consciousness.

Chapter 6: <u>The Age of Modern Taoism</u> provides an in-depth look at how contemporary mystics comprehend and define modern and ancient Tao consciousness.

Chapter 7: <u>What Is Tao consciousness?</u> explores the different stages of spiritual enlightenment.

Chapter 8: <u>Tao-Chih-Tao Poems</u> poetically describes the mysterious jade tablets that these seminal Taoist sages used both to meditate on and to train new followers. In this section I'll also explain the original mystic Taoist teachings and how you can follow the same path today to journey into the heavenly regions of clear, Tao consciousness.

Chapter 9: <u>The Tao of Ramana</u> illustrates the similarities between the primary Taoist and Sri Ramana doctrines.

Chapter 10: <u>The Golden Age of Mysticism</u> provides practical advice on how to pursue the Path of Celestial Awareness as humankind moves beyond its current chaos and toward a new era of worldwide enlightenment.

Hopefully, this book will help you to understand the true ancient path of Tao consciousness and how it might be able to guide you on your current spiritual journey as well.

CHAPTER 1

THE
AGE
OF
TRIBES

The age of tribes lasted from about 8000 BCE to 3000 BCE.

At the dawning of Chinese civilization, thousands of years *before* the emergence of the Hsia dynasty in 2205 BCE, tribal shamans were going into trances, channeling heavenly spirits, and describing those experiences to their tribes. These small nomadic, tribes were spread out over a wide territory including Siberia, Mongolia, the Turkish regions, and northern China.

The greatest shaman among these hundreds of tribes was a magically powerful man called "Yu." The next few pages tell the story of Yu.

The Spring Winds Were Late

The bitter cold winter days had ended, but the mild springtime winds were late. Far too late. The tribe was becoming restless, but the village elders didn't have any comforting answers.

The questions were endless. The answers … were empty.

Would the spring rains come before it was time to plant the crops? Or would the ground dry up, and become too parched to grow anything at all? Would the harvest be large enough to feed the village? Would their warriors have the strength to fend off the Mongol tribes that had often raided their tiny village in other lean years?

An eagle circled overhead, but the sacred cranes were flying south.

Everything, day by day and week by week, had seemed more dangerous.

And today, things seemed especially troubling. The wind was howling, louder and louder. Even in the middle of the day, the sky was dark and foreboding. The huts began to shiver and shake as the winds grew stronger.

You could hear the screams. "What is happening? Are the gods angry? Have the gods abandoned us? Did we do something wrong, to anger the gods?"

As evening crept upon the village, the sacred poles in the middle of every hut were carefully straight upward, through an opening in the roof at the largest star in the middle of the heavenly sky. The largest star that was shining brightly in the middle of the city of the gods.

But now, every family in every hut was becoming worried, and some terrified, about the increasing strength of the winds. Around the village their troubled voices could be heard: "Will the winds become strong enough to bend, or move the center-poles? And if that happens, will the gods still hear our prayers? Will they know we still love them? Will they know we still need them?"

Are we doomed without their help?

It was a small tribe of ten family huts and one larger ceremonial hut, where inside, the shaman Yu was beginning to chant.

"Praise the gods," someone yelled. "Our shaman is starting to chant. The gods can hear him, and Yu can hear the gods. Maybe he can save us."

As Yu's fire grew and clouds of smoke began to drift out of his hut, the villagers walked hopefully or ran frantically toward it. "Maybe he can find a way to please the gods!" they cried. "Maybe he can save us!"

Yu, the Greatest Shaman in the Land

"Yu, Yu!" someone yelled. "What do the gods say? Can they hear you? Will they help us?"

But the village elders silenced the crowd, got them into the hut, and persuaded them to sit down. They were still frightened. But at least there was a sliver of hope.

Their beloved shaman Yu was dancing around the fire, throwing his magic dust into the flames and causing sparks. Brilliant sparks — bright enough for the gods to see. The smoke was swirling now. Through the opening at the top of the tent, the fire was reaching up toward the heavens, begging for attention.

Photo by Alexander Nikolsky

The flames leaped larger and brighter as Yu danced around the fire, chanting his prayers louder and louder in a language that no one in the village spoke. It must be the language of the gods, they reasoned. The magical, sacred language of the gods. A tongue too sacred for a simple farmer or a soldier to understand. But Yu had been blessed by the gods, and they had taught him their language.

"Praise the gods. Praise our blessed Yu."

Yu continued beating his drum. Harder and harder as he chanted, faster and faster. Louder and louder, as he chanted in the language of the gods.

Oh, the incense. The magic incense that he threw into the fire. The incense that the gods had given him so many years ago. The magic incense that carried his sacred chants upward, swirled up and around the center pole in his tent and then out of the top of his tent and up into the heavens so the gods could hear his prayers.

The villagers were getting giddy. Their worries were becoming lighter and more distant as their shaman's magic smoke filled the entire hut. Everyone relaxed a little more.

And Yu, their beloved Yu, was talking to the gods. "Hush," one of the mothers said. "Hush, children. Be quiet so that the gods can hear his prayers. If they hear his prayers, they might save us."

Yu danced and danced as the sparks exploded in the air, and as the air became more magical. The villagers could feel the energy in the air. They could feel it on their skin. The hair on their skin rose, and an energy danced in their heads. Their bodies swayed around and around as Yu danced around the fire.

And then, suddenly, he stopped dancing. Looking up into the sky, he gasped, his mouth hanging wide open. He froze for a moment and then sat down, silently staring at something above him that no one else could see. What was it? What did he see?

After the longest moment anyone had ever experienced, Yu started talking to the gods. Talking – again in that sacred language nobody else knew. Talking softly, slowly, with a powerful reverence.

And then, he was silent. He stared into the fire, swaying back and forth, chanting a new prayer, with new words they had never heard before.

Then he stood up, chanting as he rose. Grabbing his drum again, he once again began to dance around the fire, slowly and with even greater reverence. As he danced, he glanced upward, again and again. After a few more sacred steps around the fire, he sat down and threw some more of his magic dust into the flames.

Oh my. The elders were smiling, hands together, gazing up into the heavens and trying to see the gods that were probably smiling too as they looked down upon this tiny village. As everyone began to relax, the elders knew that Yu had saved the village once again.

Yu's Legend Grew

The warm, soft spring winds came just a few days later. Because of the magical powers of their shaman, and because of the blessing of the gods, the villagers were saved once again.

With the winds and the soft rains, their small farms were safe and the tribe was able to produce a great crop.

The families were fed, and the animals were fattened. And the profits of such a great harvest helped the village to buy new farming tools and better weapons.

And news of this great miracle spread far and wide. Even before the winter harvest, villagers from other tribes were swelling the ranks of Yu's village. This strengthened the village army and brought new workers and crafts as well.

Through the ensuing years, Yu continued to accurately predict the weather patterns, the floods, and the potential attacks from marauding tribes. His prayers reached the gods, and the gods protected his village.

As the years went by, Yu's reputation among the shamans from the neighboring tribes became more impressive and more compelling.

At first his reputation spread to all the tribes within a one-day horse ride. Years later every tribe within a seven-day horse ride knew about Yu - the greatest shaman in the lands.

Eventually, this once-tiny village became known throughout the lands as the great Yubu tribe — the village where the great shaman Yu talked to the gods.

Yu felt constantly challenged to defend and demonstrate his formidable relationship with the gods. His tribe became dependent on both his capabilities and his reputation among the other tribes.

As time passed, Yu learned new skills from the gods. Among other things, they taught him how to travel to the heavens during his magical ceremonies. No other shaman could do that, although every shaman wanted to.

Every great threat the tribe faced required another face-to-face meeting in the heavens between Yu and the gods.

When disease took the life of some of the elders, Yu had to travel to the heavens to get the blessing of the gods and to get their advice on choosing and appointing new village elders. When an inter-tribal marriage was proposed, once again Yu had to go into his mystical trance and then travel in his spirit form up into the heavens to obtain the wisdom and the blessings of the gods.

On many occasions, shamans and tribal elders from nearby tribes arrived in the Yubu village to ask Yu to talk to the gods on their behalf.

He agreed, and the Yubu village became even more profitable.

Eventually, all the elders and all of Yu's potential apprentices were begging him to teach them how to travel up into the heavens as he did.

"You won't live forever," the elders said, "and we must protect the tribe. We need to think ahead. We'll be helpless if you die and leave us alone – without any way for us to talk to the gods."

Yu's apprentices agreed. "We're not as powerful as Yu. We need to be able to talk to the gods as well!"

And so, Yu, the greatest shaman in all of ancient China, fasted, chanted, prayed, and danced for three days straight. He was tired and famished but he kept on going. More chants. More drumming. More magic dust. Greater fires. Brighter sparks. Greater volumes of smoke coming out of the top of his tent and spiraling up into the heavens.

On the fourth day, the gods finally and graciously decided to teach Yu an incredible secret that he could also share with his tribe.

The Magical Steps of the Celestial Ladder

The great god Taiyi taught Yu the secret of how to fly through the celestial net and then up into the heavens.

The following diagram is a Tang dynasty Taoist rendition of the neolithic, shamanistic Yubu tribe visions that describe an early method of learning how to walk and fly the magical steps to heaven.

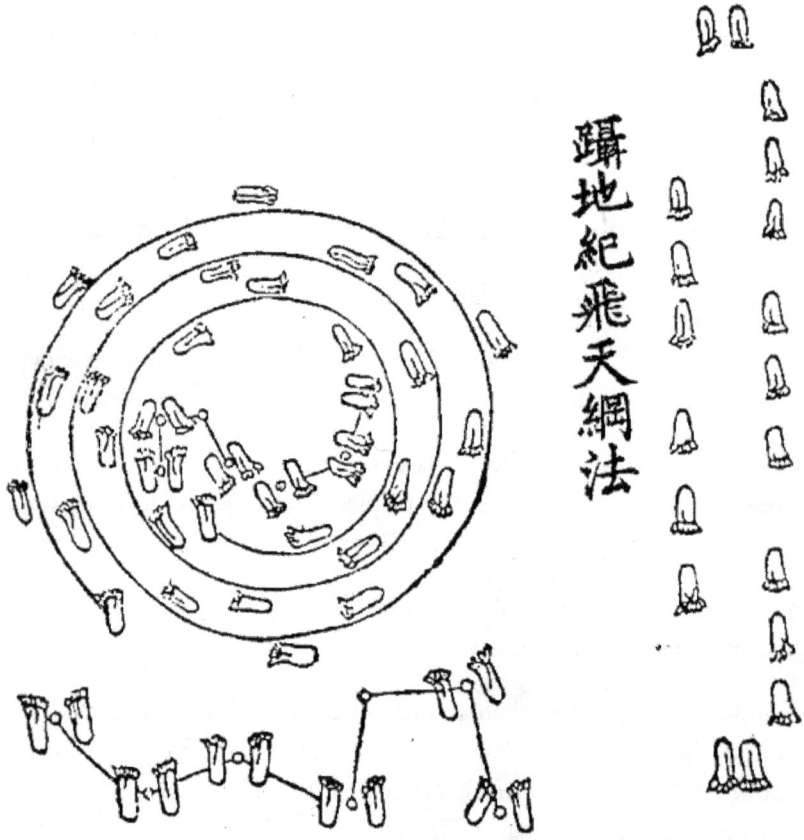

The title of this chart is *The Great One's True Secret Essentials of Helping the Tribe/Nation and Saving the People*. The footprint pattern on the right shows the steps that a Yubu tribal dancer used to lift/fly himself up into the heavens. The pattern on the upper left illustrates another path that tribal shamans could use to travel/fly up into the heavenly skies.

The center of the spiraling circle is meant to explain the importance of reaching and dissolving into the primordial breath/essence of the great Yubu god Taiyi, which would potentially grant immortality.

What a magnificent gift from the gods. What a great gift to their favorite shaman Yu. What a marvelous new way for the village elders and Yu's disciples to learn how to fly up into the heavens, and to potentially become immortal.

As the months and years rolled by, many other shamans traveled to the great Yubu tribe and learned from Yu how to dance the celestial ladder and how to talk to the gods.

But their visions and their predictions were never as accurate as Yu's predictions. And they never became immortal, or as powerful as Yu. Meanwhile, Yu was becoming even more blessed by the gods. He was becoming far more powerful.

The Year of the Great Floods

Several years after Yu had taught most of the shamans from the nearby tribes how to do the celestial dance, a new danger threatened every village within a short distance from the Yubu tribes.

The winter snows had been much heavier than anyone who was still alive could ever remember. Every peak of every large and small mountain was covered with several feet of snow.

It was beautiful to see.

But when the warm spring winds began to blow, the snow began to melt. As it melted, the river's currents became so strong that it seemed as if the gods were angry once again. So angry that it almost seemed like vengeance!

The rivers flooded down the mountains and poured over the rivers' ancient banks. Boats were destroyed. Dozens of wooden bridges were demolished, torn to bits by the angry rivers. Huts were destroyed. Entire villages were swept away, as if they had never been there before.

Throngs of frightened villagers from the neighboring tribes ran in a state of panic into Yubu to plead with Yu for his help. The entire village of Yubu was frightened as well.

However, in this instance, the great floods were only a day or so away from Yubu, and Yu didn't have time to dance for several days as he normally did.

Then, according to the ancient legends, the gods relented and sent a golden dragon down to the Yubu village in the middle of the night. In the dark of the midnight hour, Yu climbed up on the back of the dragon and immediately flew back up into the heavens to plead with the gods for help.

When he got there, the great god Taiyi taught him how to tame the angry floods, Tayi showed him how to use heavenly magic to create new channels in the mountains that would divert the torrents of melted snow away the valleys and the plains of the Yubu tribe and surrounding villages.

When Yu returned to the northwestern mountains, he used his new powers to create some new channels descending from the high mountain lakes. As a result of this magical gift from the gods, waterfalls were created, forming new golden lakes and new golden rivers that safely ran through the Yubu lands without endangering the Yubu villages or their inhabitants.

In the years that followed, many of the greatest shamans in the land reported seeing additional yellow dragons in the mountainous regions. They emerged from the golden lakes and the yellow rivers, flying upward into the heavenly skies.

Everyone marveled at this great gift from Taiyi and from his favorite shaman Yu. Over the years the tales of yellow dragon grew throughout the land. In every village, in every valley, and in every mountain town, everyone had heard at least three or four different tales about these magical yellow dragons.

The Dragon Gate

Far into the northwest regions of the tallest mountains anyone had ever seen, there was a great mountain that Yu had split in two to create a channel through which the Yellow River could flow.

This is a famous painting about the Dragon Gate at the top of the mountain. Today, the Yellow River of ancient times still flows though the Dragon Gate at the top of this mountain pass.

This mountain was so high that it reached above the white clouds and above the swirling winds that the yellow dragons used on their flight up into the heavens. It was so high that its waterfalls crashed down upon the rocks below and created new lakes. These huge lakes eventually flowed from the mountains to become powerful yellow rivers full of fish that helped to feed the Yubu villages along the sides of the rivers.

Such a precious gift from the gods. Such a magnificent gift from the greatest shaman in the lands. Such a splendid gift from Yu.

In ancient times, every year in the spring carp travel up from the sea and swim in huge numbers in the pool at the bottom of this majestic waterfall.

Shortly after arriving, they would then try to swim up the waterfall and past the yellow dragon gate at the top of the mountain.

The fables say that only a few rare fish are mystically destined to be able to swim up the waterfall. The first fish that swims through the dragon gate, is transformed into a powerful yellow dragon, which then magically enables the spring rains to fall.

The ancient legends say that throughout the ages, there has always been a great immortal yellow dragon that lives at the top of the mountain. Apparently, this dragon often appears and then magically disappears, only to appear again in a different location. Truly magical. Truly immortal.

Everyone wants to believe in something special, until it doesn't seem special anymore. That's when many people stop believing. The key is to continue believing even when things seem ordinary.

Most of the shamans were "secretly" claiming to be able to follow the yellow dragons up into the heavens – even though they knew that they didn't know what heaven was actually like.

To every shaman and every Yubu villager, heaven was mostly just an empty dream.

CHAPTER 2

THE
AGE
OF
MYSTICS

The Age of Mystics lasted from 5000 BCE to 2200 BCE.

The ancient beliefs about magical, immortal, yellow dragons became an integral part of ancient Chinese culture. In fact, the ancient belief in magical dragons is still prevalent today in modern China.

The image of the yellow dragon is still a precious symbol of the magical strength and the immortal ways of the Chinese civilization.

Statues, etchings, and pictures of dragons are ubiquitous in modern China. You can find them on thousands of Taoist temples, museum walls, artwork, etchings, book covers, and posters. And they remind us of the precious heart of Chinese culture.

The Evolution of Ancient Wisdom

Throughout the entire early history of ancient and medieval China, tribal shaman beliefs had a significant impact on emerging Chinese mystic paths, religions, and philosophies.

The formative centuries of China's great civilization began with hundreds of tiny villages like Yubu and with legendary shamans like Yu. The oldest villages evolved from tiny nomadic tribes around 7000 BCE to large established villages in 5000 BCE and then to bustling cities that dotted the map of China around 2500 BCE.

During this entire period, the nomadic tribes traveled throughout the lands, listening to every legend, and sharing every legend with every village they encountered.

The decisive moment of growth of the Chinese civilization occurred around 2200 BCE with the establishment of the Hsia dynasty — the first dynasty in China.

But Chinese culture and history actually began to evolve long before that, from 7000–200 BCE, with its craftsmen, elders, shamans, and Taoist sages. The early shamanistic beliefs and Taoist meditation practices coexisted, and they often heavily influenced the eventual philosophical, cultural, and spiritual beliefs of every dynasty in ancient China.

The advent of shamans, and their magico-religious visions, at the dawning of most great civilizations, has had a tremendous impact on many of the greatest religions on Earth.

Shamans were not madmen, or charlatans. They weren't dope addicts or crazed magicians. They were trained wisdom teachers who knew how to enter psychic trances and talk with various godlike spirits.

They had celestial visions about cosmology and the ways of the gods, and Earthly visions about practical things that affected their tribes. They had visions about new weather patterns and potential wars, visions about fertility and death, and important visions about everyday issues that most tribal members worried about.

The vitality and daily life of most tribes revolved around the shamans, and their religious beliefs.

According to Mircea Eliade in her classic book *Shamanism: Archaic Techniques of Ecstasy* the ancient Neolithic tribes shared numerous common cross-cultural themes.

The ancient Siberian, Mongolian, and Northern Chinese tribes followed this same pattern of cultural themes in common. Moreover, many of their most basic "spiritual" convictions lasted for thousands of years and were integrated into a wide range of emergent Chinese, and worldwide religions, philosophies, and mystic paths.

The most influential tribal beliefs in ancient China included myths about the creation of the Earth by the gods in the sky, and more important, myths about legendary shamans and the yellow dragons who knew the secret ways to fly from Earth and into the center of the celestial heavens.

The Enduring Legend of the Yellow Dragon

During the early period of the mystical Taoist path, the yellow dragon became a precious symbol for both a fully enlightened Taoist sage and for the creative consciousness within every Taoist disciple.

Based on their wisdom teachings, the ancient Taoist sages would have reached the crown chakra stage of consciousness. This region of consciousness is conspicuous for its bright, radiant golden light, which is at least one hundred times brighter than the sun. Thus, a Taoist monk was probably pronounced as a Taoist sage after having visited the crown region of consciousness. The ancient word *huang* means "yellow" as well as "radiant" — which would symbolically connect the accomplished yellow dragon Taoist Sage with the sun as the center part of the universe. In deep states of clear awareness, there is often a golden glow surrounding the meditator, thereby proving that the monk had reached the state of the fabled yellow dragon.

The disappearance of the entire physical body, for short periods of time, is another common experience, among meditators who have reached the crown chakra. Thus, if a Taoist sage disappeared while meditating in front of his students, most students would probably assume that their teacher was as immortal as the legendary yellow dragons.

As the legends of Taoist Immortals and their divine powers grew, the imperial families borrowed the yellow dragon symbol as well. The yellow dragon eventually became the familiar imperial symbol of the emperor of China.

The Chinese dragon has thus become an auspicious symbol of great and benevolent, magical power. The image of a carp jumping over the Dragon Gate is another related and enduring Chinese cultural symbol for courage, strength, concentration, perseverance, and accomplishment.

The symbol of the yellow dragon continued to grow over time until it became legendary. The yellow dragon is now a pervasive, enduring symbol of prestige, pride and accomplishment throughout the entirety of Chinese culture.

One of the most common Chinese proverbs heard today in modern China is "The carp has leaped through the dragon's gate." To this day, when a student passes the rigorous national university examination in China, friends and family proudly gather to sing the cheer "LIYU TIAO LONG MEN!"

Tribal Shamans

Even after the Age of Tribes and the Age of Mystics, shaman mysticism coexisted with the religions and philosophies in the Age of Emperors and their dynasties. As Chinese civilization began to establish itself in the Hsia, Shang, and Zhou dynasties, the tribal shaman beliefs became even more prevalent, often heavily influencing the beliefs and teachings of early religious, philosophical, Confucian, and Taoist paths.

The advent of shamans, and their magico-religious visions, at the dawning of most great civilizations, has had a tremendous impact on many of the greatest religions on Earth.

Many of their most basic "spiritual" convictions lasted for thousands of years and were eventually integrated into a wide range of emergent Chinese, and worldwide, religions, philosophies, and mystic paths.

The Creation Myths of Shamans

The root of the word *shaman* comes to us from the nomadic tribes in the Siberian regions of modern-day Russia. In the Siberian Tungusic language, the word *saman* was used to describe tribal mystics. In China the word *shaman* was used instead of the Siberian term *saman*. But the role of shamans was very similar across all the northern and western regions of Asia.

Local nomadic tribes were spread throughout all the ancient lands that made up central and north Asia. Most of these earliest shamanistic tribes were centered on hunting and fishing activities. Farming and ranching activities began to spring up as early as 7000 BCE.

It was always the mystic shaman who was responsible for the magical visions about cosmology, creation, and the will of the gods. Most tribal villagers firmly believed the visions, the myths, and the ideology of their beloved shamans.

Both the shamans and villagers religiously believed in a group of celestial gods and a great god who was the all-powerful creator of everything. Sometimes, the name of that great god also meant "sky" or "heaven." Tengri was the great god of the Mongols, and Taiyi was the great god of the Yubu and many other Chinese tribes.

Whatever the great god was called, the ancient creation legends of tribal shamans started with myths about heavenly gods that lived in the sky and created the Earth, all of the mountains and valleys of Earth, and all the men on Earth and all other creatures on Earth. They also believed that these sky gods controlled the weather and the fates of humans, but their magical shamans could talk with and get help from these heavenly gods. And Yu was widely regarded as the greatest shaman in the Chinese lands.

These were the primary spiritual beliefs among the shamanistic tribes, for thousands of years in ancient China.

The Evolution of Great Saints

Throughout the ages on Earth most of the greatest saints were either born with divine wisdom or became divinely wise at an early age. This includes saints like Buddha, Krishna, Christ, Kabir, Guru Nanak, and Kirpal. Heavenly, spiritual wisdom at an early age seems to be an essential foundation of most of the great saints that eventually created large worldwide spiritual paths and religions.

Moreover, most great saints used the common widely followed belief systems of their region to build their new faith. It's much easier to explain deep truths about a mystic consciousness path if you start with an analysis of the mystic wisdom that was "always hidden" within the common myths and doctrines of the local population.

For example, Buddha used the ancient Pali and Vedic doctrine of Tathagata (heavenly awareness) as a starting point for his teachings. Yeshua

(Jesus Christ) used the local Gnostic (mystic consciousness) teachings to explain his wisdom path. Kabir and other Indian gurus like Ramana used the local Vedic doctrines to explain their I-AM consciousness paths. The great mid-Eastern Sufi saints like Hafiz and Rumi employed the regional teachings of Mohammed as a foundational element of their mystic poems and doctrine.

My path was similar. I was blessed with a deep comprehension of divine consciousness as a child, and I have used the teachings of many of these great saints mentioned above to explain non-cognitive consciousness and the path to Celestial Awareness to other seekers.

Likewise, Bodhidharma, a famous monk in the fifth or sixth century CE, used his Buddhist Indian training on pure awareness — compared to ancient Taoist wisdom — to develop the Chan path of direct consciousness in China — which later became the Zen path of silent consciousness in Japan.

And somewhere in ancient China a great saint was most likely born with a significant level of divine consciousness, who borrowed the pre-existing shaman creation myths as a starting point for their initial teachings about Tao consciousness.

The Origin of Ancient, Mystic Taoism

It's impossible to know the exact date and place that Taoism began. However, the earliest "oral" ancient Taoist teachings most likely began during the Age of Tribes between approximately 5500–4000 BCE. This estimate is primarily based on Chinese archaeological excavations that discovered hundreds of jade Taoist tablets that were carved during this ancient time frame. Hundreds of additional jade tablets, dating from 4000–1000 BCE, were also excavated in other archaeological digs.

As evidenced by the following diagram, many of these jade tablets were uncovered in buildings and in ancient graves.

Because some of these tablets were found in graves, the earliest archaeologists guessed that the jade tablets were functionally like the Egyptian tablets that were placed in the coffins of Egyptian kings to guide them on their way to heaven. These scientists might have been partially correct. Some of the jade tablets might have been left by tribal villagers, familiar with the ancient Taoist teachings to help their relatives travel to heaven.

However, it's evident that the earliest Taoist tablets were also used to teach pre-dynasty Chinese villagers about the nature of Tao consciousness, Tao cosmology, how to meditate on Tao consciousness, and how to travel inward as a Taoist toward heavenly consciousness.

The Taoist Heaven and Earth Jade Tablet

The Taoist Jade Tablet pictured above was created somewhere between 6000 BCE and 5000 BCE, which makes it the oldest written spiritual teaching on Earth.

The center of the stone represents the original, celestial, state of Tao consciousness. It is the original, pure state of the Tao consciousness – the cosmic awareness that exists before, during, and after the created cosmos. It is also called the undifferentiated void. It still exists – as the creator and the essence of all things.

The ring-shaped surface of the jade tablet represents the manifest Earth/cosmos. It is the essence of the cosmos and all of the heavens as well as the Earth and all the ten thousand things on Earth. Everything that was created by Tao is still within cosmic Tao consciousness and contains the same celestial consciousness within it.

The Original Wu Wei Taoist Teaching

The straight horizontal line was deliberately carved across the middle of this jade tablet. It represents the horizon that separates the Earth from the heavens.

This line is also meant to show the counterbalancing yin/yang effect that governs all forms of life on Earth and in the heavens. The empty hole in the center represents Tao consciousness as well as the middle way beyond all positive and negative events in life. Please note that the yin/yang line does not cut through the empty circle. On most later yin/yang jade tablets the horizontal line was etched just below the empty circle.

This seven-thousand-year-old jade tablet was not only used to teach the Taoist creation cosmology but was also used to teach the basic principles of wu wei and how to effortlessly float through life in a wu wei state of Tao consciousness.

The Taoist Version of the Yellow Dragon

The Yubu villagers didn't know it at this time, but after many years this legend became the inspiration for the new emerging Taoist Path of the Yellow Dragon (Huang-Long).

The yellow dragon was initially defined as the Taoist monk, or sage, that is filled with the magical, immortal, power of Tao consciousness.

The following translucent jade tablet depicts an ancient Taoist yellow dragon sage that is filled with magical Taoist energy of spiraling Ki seeds. The ki seeds, in ancient times, were believed to contain the magical powers and the vital essence that enabled the legendary yellow dragons to fly from the Earth to the heavens.

The above tablet, like the following tablet, was carved somewhere between 5000 BCE and 2500 BCE.

The Taoist Version of the Way to Heaven

Sometimes the ancient Taoists used jade tablets carved in the shape of a yellow dragon. However, when they were explaining the Taoist version of the "Way to Heaven," they would etch a portrait of the yellow dragon onto the surface of the tablet.

The following beautiful translucent jade tablet was used to teach the secret Taoist path, or way, to heavenly consciousness.

The tablet was meant to convey the idea that any Taoist monk or student, who learns how to discover and hold on to Tao consciousness will become just like the fabled yellow dragon that can easily fly from the

Earth and up into the celestial sky —which is the true source and creator of the ten thousand things.

Because the Taoist teachers, or sages, had mastered the technique of floating effortlessly in Tao consciousness, they were therefore the living examples of the fabled yellow dragons. And because they had also reached heavenly consciousness, they could teach other monks how to find and travel the secret ways to heaven.

The empty vertical space that runs from the outer edge of the tablet to its empty center was used to teach that a constant certainty of Tao consciousness is necessary to travel the entire path from human awareness to Celestial Awareness.

This clear awareness path to celestial Taoist consciousness also becomes a much easier path to follow than any other path, because Tao awareness, once achieved, is always beyond yin/yang duality. Yellow dragon consciousness, signified by the etched yellow dragon on the (Earthly) surface of this tablet, teaches the monks that Tao consciousness obscures and dissolves all karmic problems and related yin/yang energy patterns.

During the early years of the mystical Taoist path, the yellow dragon became a precious symbol for both a fully enlightened Taoist sage and for the creative consciousness within every Taoist disciple.

The Taoist Version of the Celestial Net

In Chapter 1, the Age of Tribes, we talked about how the ancient shamans, like Yu, knew the secret ways beyond the celestial net that would otherwise trap or prevent anyone except the shamans from entering the heavens. The shamans, however, were gifted with the knowledge of the way to heaven and knew how to travel there.

The ancient Taoist version of the celestial net is illustrated on the Taoist tablet that follows.

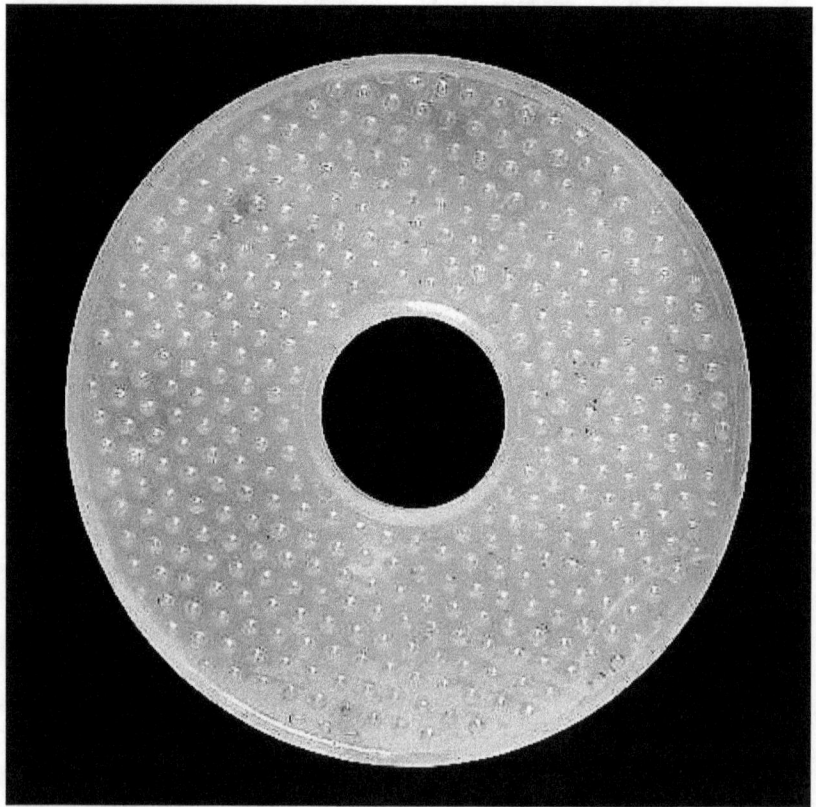

The center of this Jade Taoist disk represents the primordial, heavenly essence of Tao consciousness. The numerous bumps on the surface of the tablet represent the interconnection points between counterbalanced positive and negative energy.

You could also say, in Western lingo, that these bumps represent the points in time and space where your desire-based and fear-based karma is interconnected. Every time that you begin to run away, or look away from, fear-based karma and automatically run, or look toward desires that make you forget your karma, you arrive at one of these interconnection points.

The surface of this disk represents the virtual-matrix net of karma that we must learn to go beyond by meditating on Tao consciousness. After moving beyond this karmic net, we have the potential to discover and melt into the immortal Tao consciousness at the center of our soul.

The Path of the Yellow Dragon

Based on the evidence we have that these ancient Taoist tablets teach the earliest Taoist wisdom during or slightly after the formative years of tribal Chinese shaman beliefs, we can state with confidence that ancient Taoism is the oldest, most consistently followed spiritual path in the world.

Moreover, it is unquestionably the oldest religious/mystic path that is still followed today on Earth. It has changed in many ways since the earliest Ways of Heaven era, but in other ways, the most essential Taoist doctrines have not changed at all.

Inward-focused Taoist meditation practices, that enable monks to go beyond mind-body awareness to eventually discover celestial awareness were not only at the core of these ancient teachings, but also at the center of most direct awareness doctrines taught by fully enlightened, contemporary mystics like Nan Huai-chin, Ramana, Nisargadatta, and me.

It was because of sacred Taoist tablets like this that we know the Taoist saints were often called *yu shih*—which means "jade sage" in Old

Chinese. In the early days of the Taoist path, it was most likely referred to as *huang long*, or the Path of the Yellow Dragon.

CHAPTER 3

THE
AGE
OF
EMPERORS

1776–220 BCE

The Hsia, or Xia, dynasty was the first dynasty in ancient China. Hsia was established in 1766 BCE by the legendary Emperor Yu. According to ancient legends, Yu was able to tame the Yellow River and prevent flooding.

The Shang dynasty began when a tribal chief named Tang defeated the Hsia dynasty in 1600 BCE. The Shang dynasty was ultimately conquered by the Zhou dynasty in 1045 BCE.

The Zhou dynasty, which ruled for 789 years until 220 BCE, was the longest dynastic regime in Chinese history.

The Tao consciousness path flourished in all three dynasties.

The Dawning of Chinese Civilization

During most of the twentieth century, the most popular theory about the cradle of civilization on Earth was that it started in the Fertile Crescent, expanding from there to the rest of the world. The Fertile Crescent included numerous small settlements in and around the Nile Valley and the Tigris–Euphrates Valley in North Africa and the Middle East.

However, numerous, recent, scientific, and scholarly studies have convincingly demonstrated that several different cradles of civilization arose independently at several locations around the world in the early Neolithic era (10000 to 7000 BCE).

The Chinese civilization was one of these first great "cradles of civilization" in the world. This early Chinese culture grew up around various Neolithic settlements located near or between the northern Yellow River and the southern Yangzi River. Chinese civilization flourished in both farming and nomadic villages.

Throughout the entire Neolithic era (10000 to 3000 BCE), the sedentary and nomadic communities continually shared various tribal beliefs, shamanic visions, language, and trading goods.

The earliest evidence of Chinese millet agriculture is dated to around 7000 BCE, and the earliest evidence of cultivated rice occurred around 6500 BCE. Millet and rice farming enabled population growth and crop storage; and it fostered a growing class of specialized craftsmen, which in turn led to the development of better weapons, tools, pottery, and jade tablets.

According to the Metropolitan Museum of Art in New York City, these early settlements "relied primarily on farming and domesticated animals." The key archaeologists at the Met also believe that these early settlements "independently developed their own cultural traditions, creating distinctive kinds of architecture, and customs, but with some communication and cultural exchange between them."

Some archeologists and scholars have suggested that the Jiahu (a Neolithic cultural site in Henan, China) cave drawing symbols (6600 BCE) excavated in 1989 and the Jade tablet pictograms (5000 BCE) were the earliest forms of written language in China. However, it is more sensible to view the cave drawings and jade pictograms as "early symbols" that eventually led to the Old Chinese system of writing.

In this photo, an archaeologist points to an ancient Jiahu cave drawing, estimated to be at least seven thousand years old, with a pictogram of

the sun. About two thousand years later, many jade tablets appeared with similar pictograms of the same Chinese word.

Like most other civilizations that developed during this era, the Neolithic Chinese culture produced and left behind a wide variety of pottery, tools, utensils, weapons and ornaments.

Jade was discovered and mined in the early years of the emerging Chinese civilization. Initially jade was primarily used to create primitive farming tools and weapons.

However, it was the mining of jade and the subsequent carving of jade pictograms that were later used to record and teach ancient mystical Taoism that so greatly distinguished the accomplishments of this early Chinese civilization.

Guang Chengzi and the Yellow Emperor

The earliest official mention of the ancient Taoist path comes from the philosopher Chuang Tzu who was a renowned associate and follower of Lao Tzu. According to Chuang Tzu, an ancient Taoist sage named Guang Chengzi was the initial avatar of the original Taoist path.

Chuang Tzu also describes the journey that the Yellow Emperor, Huang Di, took to the sacred Kong Tong mountains, to be trained by Guang Chengzi on the key principles and practices of ancient Taoism.

Xuan Yuan (Yellow Emperor) Inquires of the Dao,

National Palace Museum, Taipei, Taiwan

Although there are numerous fables about his achievements, and his relationships with the gods, the Yellow Emperor is widely regarded as a historical figure in Chinese culture. He is believed to have been the original inventor of traditional Chinese music, medicine, the calendar, and much more.

Apparently, Guang Chengzi also helped Huang Di by giving him three different books that helped him to create the Chinese language, rules of conduct, and philosophical principles.

According to Chuang Tzu, the immortal Taoist avatar Guang Chengzi had lived for over twelve hundred years and had appeared three times. Chuang noted that he first appeared as Guang Chengzi in ancient times, next as Lao Tzu in the Spring and Autumn period, and for the third time as Zhang Daoling in the Han dynasty.

Huang-Di first became the ruling Yellow Emperor in 2698 BCE, indicating that Guang Chengzi was born at least twenty to fifty years before the Yellow Emperor's rule.

This fact alone shows that the path of Tao consciousness was established before 2697 BCE. But as we know from looking at the age of the oldest Taoist Jade tablets, the Taoist path was originally established before 5000 BCE.

The Origin of Ancient, Mystic Taoism

As mentioned in the previous chapter, the initial Taoist path of the Yellow Dragon began around 5000 BCE. This is more than two thousand years before the reign of the Yellow Emperor, which also indicates that Guang Chengzi could not have been the true founder of the Taoist path. Thus, we don't know the identity of the true founder of the Path of the Yellow Dragon, but at least we have a reasonable estimate of when the path began.

The earliest oral ancient Taoist teachings most likely began shortly before or after the production of the first jade Taoist tablets, which were created somewhere between 6000 BCE and 4500 BCE.

Many of the fables about the Yellow Emperor mention that he traveled around his empire in an ivory chariot pulled by yellow dragons. This would seem to indicate that during the time of the Yellow Emperor, the initial Taoist path was still using symbolic references to the magical yellow dragons.

During the Golden Age of Taoism (770–221 BCE) near the end of the Zhou Empire, the Taoist terminology had changed, and there were few references to be found about yellow dragons.

The Kuan-Tzu text on inward training talked about Tao as the *vital essence* or as the *One*. The Zuang-zi described Tao as the *primordial energy*, or qi, that created the cosmos and humankind. Lao Tzu talked about Tao as the way of *Virtue* or simply as *Tao*. Han Feizi, who reportedly composed about one-third of the Tao Te Ching, depicted Tao as either the *Way* or the *Source*.

It seems obvious that (1) the terminology used to describe this ancient direct-awareness path changed over time and (2) there was an increasing emphasis on inward-training meditation practices instead of training new monks to symbolically emulate the nature of the sacred yellow dragons.

Over the centuries there was also increasing importance placed on conscious teachings instead of the legendary comparisons to the fables about yellow dragons. The Taoist path flourished during the Hsia, Shang, and Zhou dynasties even though the terminology changed over time.

The Shang dynasty was crucial to the initial development of the Taoist teachings. This dynasty was responsible for (1) the introduction of jade mining and carving, (2) the production of several important jade Taoist tablets, (3) the introduction of early Taoist cosmology, and (4) the widespread distribution of myths about immortal yellow dragons and Taoist sages.

It was during the Zhou dynasty, however, that Taoism became a popular mystic path and eventually a widespread Chinese philosophy. It was the development of the well-defined, widely accepted, Old Chinese language combined with the refined production of Jade tablets, that enabled and empowered the growth of the Taoist path.

Taoist Teachings during the Shang Dynasty

The Shang dynasty not only introduced jade mining technology and significantly contributed to the development of jade tablets, ornaments, and pottery; it was instrumental in the emerging Bronze Age in China. Based on an examination of ancient tortoise-shell inscriptions and other documents, most archaeologists believe that Shang-Dynasty scientists and other scholars were not only using calendars, but they had also developed a fundamental grasp of math, astronomy, and the Old Chinese language. They were also known for their significant advances in art and military technology.

During the Shang dynasty, the master artisans were creating sophisticated bronze works as well as jade ceramics, jewelry, meditation stones, and Taoist jade tablets. Unlike the earlier era, the Shang Dynasty artisans utilized piece-mold casting as opposed to the lost-wax method. This enabled the jade sages to hire artisans who could easily and quickly create the jade tablets they used for teaching.

The Yin Ruins Museum at Anyang, Henan, appropriately celebrates and honors the cultural, historical, and spiritual artifacts from the last capital of the great Chinese Shang dynasty.

The museum has an excellent collection of the oldest known archaic Chinese writings on oracle bones as well as an impressive collection of ancient pottery, bronze vessels, jade tablets, and other unearthed cultural relics. The gateway to the museum honors the spiritual significance of the yellow dragon to Shang-dynasty rulers, to Taoist sages, and to modern Chinese culture.

As evidenced by the teachings themselves, the Taoist mystics were great saints who had reached the highest levels of heavenly consciousness. Moreover, they had continual access to skilled artisans who could easily carve the jade tablets that the Jade sages needed for their teaching.

It was also significant that the Shang people already seemed to have a strong reverence for mystical stories, yellow dragons, immortal sages, creation fables, and other heavenly teachings.

Within the higher echelon of the Shang society, the king presented himself as a spiritual priest. This king/priest led in the worship of Shangdi – the supreme heavenly ancestor. Many scholars believe that according to Chinese legends, Shang ancestors were in direct communication with the god Di. The ancestors' instructions were first received by a group of mystics and then presented by the king.

Despite the great achievements of the Shang dynasty, these were brutal times for the general population. Humans were often sacrificed in religious ceremonies by the king and his imperial priests.

Apparently, during the ancient era in the Shang dynasty, most of the great mystic teachings were never written down. They were taught orally to their disciples and passed on in a similar manner from one great sage to another.

Development of the Chinese Language

Most professional linguists and scholars agree that the modern Chinese language is at least three thousand years old – making Mandarin the oldest written and spoken language in current use on Earth.

They also suggest that this language initially evolved from a language they refer to as either Old Chinese or Archaic Chinese.

Linguist scholars William H. Baxter and Laurent Sagart refer to Old Chinese as the "varieties of Chinese dialects used before the eventual unification of China under the Qin dynasty in 221 BC."

Archaic Chinese, as a complete spoken and written language, appears to date back to about 1200 BC. Two of the most important initial discoveries in China were the archaeological dig that uncovered the Jiaguwen-script oracle bone and shell inscriptions found at Anwang that were used during the reign of the late Shang-dynasty king Wu Ding. These were pivotal discoveries that led most sinologists (language experts) to the conclusion that Old Chinese first became a unified and standardized language around this time.

Ancient Chinese Pictograms

There are about seven thousand ideogram characters in the modern Chinese language. These characters are arranged in various ways to create approximately 106,000 different Chinese characters and words.

Most sinologists believe that the first characters and words used around 1200 BCE evolved both from primitive symbols and drawings found in caves, as well as from jade tablets. Depending on which scientists you believe, the cave drawings were created in the Neolithic Age, somewhere between 12000 BCE and approximately 3000 BCE.

Archaic Chinese also evolved both from much earlier cave-drawing symbols and from jadestone pictograms. The current belief among language scholars is that the Old Chinese language most likely centered on only a few hundred pictograms that were commonly used during the Shang dynasty.

There is no convincing evidence of any phonetic use or known words that would be necessary to produce a complete functional script as seen in the Shang dynasty's oracle-bone script.

Leading Chinese scholar Qiu Xigui has said that "these symbols definitely cannot be considered as a fully formed system of writing; this much is quite clear. We simply possess no basis for saying that they were already being used to record language."

The earliest jade bi tablets were created thousands of years after the earliest cave drawings. The pictograms on these early jade-bi tablets have been scientifically dated to about 5000 BCE and most likely represent some of the earliest pictograms in the Archaic Chinese language.

Unfortunately, these earliest Old Chinese pictograms faded into obscurity when the Mandarin script was modernized.

Circles versus Squares and Lines

Eventually, the early Chinese scribes who created the first "official" characters of the Old Chinese language in the emerging Zhou dynasty incorporated the original characters of the jade-bi stones. However, they also eliminated all the original jade-bi pictogram circles and replaced them with squares, straight lines, and slightly curved lines.

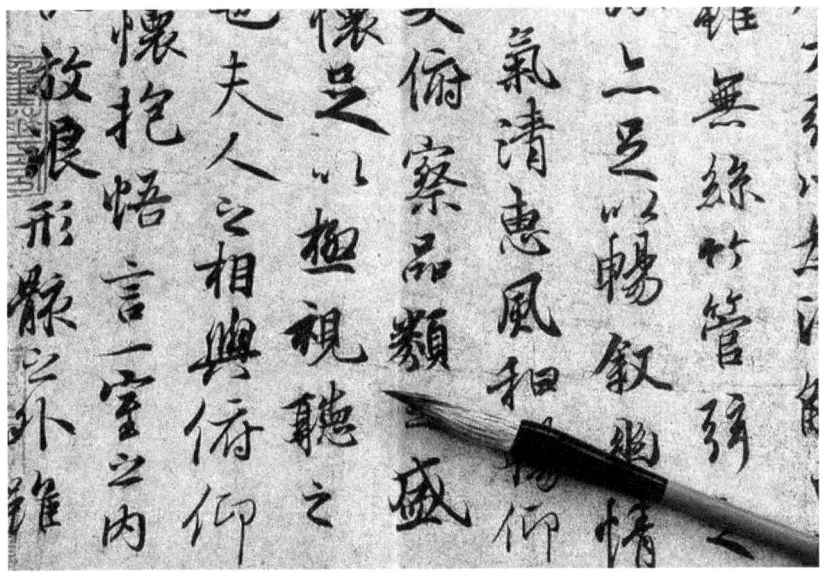

Apparently, it was much easier and faster for the ancient scribes to draw a square instead of a perfectly round circle.

That single decision by some unknown court scribe created some incredible misconceptions. Because the circles of these original characters never appear in the modern Chinese language, thousands of later language scholars, historians, and philosophers failed to see the linguistic and mystic importance of these early jade-bi tablets.

Because they failed to see that these ancient jade pictograms were words as well as precious statements of mystical wisdom, future scholars also failed to recognize that they were (1) one of the most important original sources of the Chinese language, (2) the beginning of the Chinese language, and (3) the beginning of ancient mystical Taoism.

The Forgotten Ancient Taoist Tablets

The earliest Taoist scripture consisted of pictograms that were either carved jade tablets, or etchings on carved jade tablets during the Age of Tribes and later in the HSIA and Shang Dynasties. Hundreds of jade tablets have recently been discovered by archaeologists, but the mystic wisdom was simply not obvious to scientists.

The Shang dynasty was crucial to the initial development of the Taoist teachings. This dynasty was responsible for (1) the introduction of jade mining and carving, (2) the production of several important jade Taoist tablets, (3) the introduction of early Taoist cosmology, and (4) the widespread myths about immortal yellow dragons and Taoist sages.

It was during the Zhou Dynasty, however, that Taoism became a popular mystic path and eventually a widespread Chinese philosophy. It was the development of the well-defined, widely accepted Old Chinese language, in combination with the refined production of jade tablets, that enabled and empowered the growth of the Taoist path.

Worldwide Power Struggles

Throughout the entire ancient world from 3000–100 BCE, war, the threat of war, and preparation for wars became one of the highest single priorities for every nation, state, empire, and dynasty.

It was true in China. It was also true throughout Asia, Russia, the Far East, the Mideast, Africa, Europe, and most other parts of the world.

During this period, hundreds of major wars involving thousands of soldiers were fought in Egypt, Babylon, Uruk, Nubia, Sumeria, Kish, Akkadia, Mesopotamia, Assyria, Anatolia, Turkey, Persia, India, Greece, Rome, China, Siberia, Mongolia, Aram, Israel, Sparta, Judah, Gandhara, Iran, Iraq, Lydia, Cyprus, Carthage, Gallia, Macedonia, Maurya, Parthia, Hispania, Syria, Armenia, Albania, and many other nations. It was a worldwide era of poverty, revolts, revolutions, and imperial conquest.

In every nation, the most important duty of kings, rulers, and emperors was ostensibly to protect their civilization and the welfare of their people. Because of the constant threats of military conflict, most of these leaders tended to rule with an iron fist, and thus they were often ruthless toward not only their political rivals but any other formidable religious or social organizations that threatened them.

The Chinese Mandate of Heaven

In China, things were no different. Chinese history from ancient times to pre-modern times is, to a great extent, a succession of powerful dynasties with new rulers but with little change in language, society, culture, and religion.

Chinese emperors were no different from the kings and rulers of most other nations and empires in ancient times. They always had to keep their empire prepared for war.

New rulers would do whatever they felt was necessary to protect their legitimate right and ability to rule – while trying to avoid causing too much upheaval among the populace.

Accordingly, few major changes occurred within the general society. There were frequent transitions related to the spoken and written languages but few alterations to social or cultural trends.

However, starting with the first emperor of the Zhou dynasty, Wu Wang, every newly formed dynasty used what was called the "Mandate of Heaven" to justify their moral and divine right to destroy the previous empire and to establish their legitimate right to rule.

Emperor Wu Wang was the first king in China to claim the Mandate of Heaven when he established the new Zhou dynasty. The Mandate of Heaven was described as a Heavenly proclamation by the supreme god in heaven to justify, support, and mandate the moral superiority and rule of the new dynasty.

Wu Wang contended that heaven had blessed his dynasty's triumph because the previous Shang emperors had been evil men whose policies brought pain to the people through waste and corruption.

It was easy to describe the last emperor of the Shang dynasty, King Di Xing, as evil. Di Xing had a reputation as a cruel leader who enjoyed punishing and torturing his slaves, his soldiers, and his citizens. In the last battle with the incoming Zhou dynasty army, historians say that more than two hundred thousand slaves and soldiers defected to Zhou forces.

Di Xing then committed suicide by setting fire to his own palace, killing himself and many other innocent people.

As explained in Wikipedia on the Dynastic Cycle page, "There is a famous Chinese proverb expressed in the 16th-century novel *Romance of the Three Kingdoms* that says, "After a long split, a union will occur; after a long union, a split will occur" (分久必合，合久必分). Each of these rulers would claim the *Mandate of Heaven* to legitimize their rule."

And it all began with the rise of the Zhou dynasty, during which new major imperial claims of a heavenly mandate were followed by minor changes within the general culture.

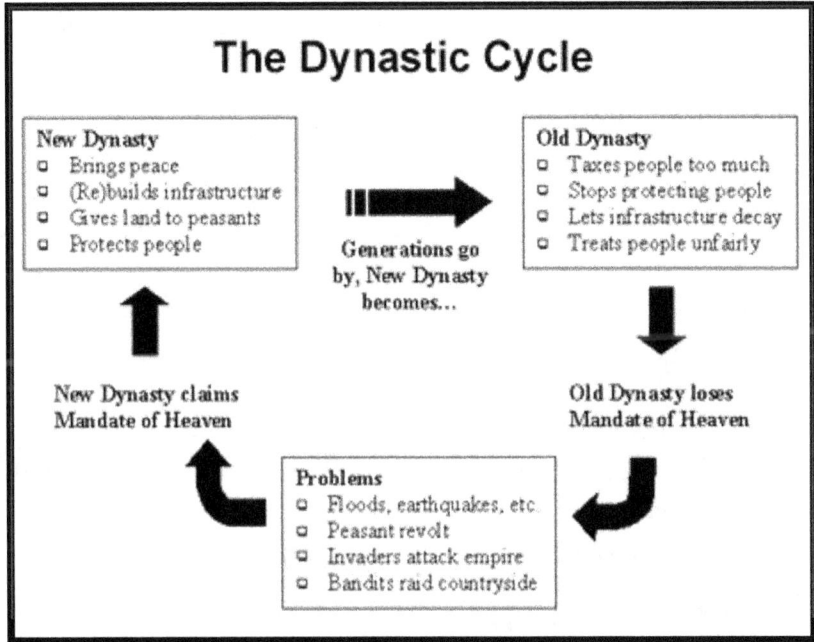

Throughout the subsequent eight-hundred-year reign of the Zhou dynasty, and the ensuing years of the Qin and Han dynasties, the Mandate of Heaven was used by the ruling classes to both demand obedience from peasants, the intellectuals, and Taoists and to "rightfully" punish any and all offenders.

The Legalist Philosophy

The Chinese philosophical school of Legalism attained prominence during the Warring States era (475–221 BCE) through the writings and influence of the Legalist philosophers Shang Yang, Li Si, and Han Feize.

The three main principles of Legalism are the strict application of widely publicized laws, the application of stringent management techniques, and the strict accountability and enforcement of imperial and dynastic law.

The Legalists believed that most humans in political and religious organizations were inherently selfish and short-sighted and thus potentially troublesome to imperial rule. They also believed that in these war times, absolute obedience to dynastic authority and social harmony could only be achieved through strong state control. They stressed the vital importance of implementing policies and laws that increased the power of the dynasty rulers and decreased the authority of religious groups.

Shang Yang and Han Feize

The two Legalist philosophers who had the greatest impact on Taoism were Shang Yang and Han Feize.

Shang Yang's greatest and most influential work was his book entitled *The book of the Lord of Shang*. This single book significantly changed the attitudes and subsequent laws of the dynasty rulers in the Han and Qin dynasties.

Han Feize was not only a renowned Legalist philosopher, but he was also a member of the Han Royal Family. Like Shang Yang, Han Feize heavily influenced the Han and Qin dynasty implementations of new laws and dynasty management techniques that were based on Legalist philosophies.

Conflicts with the Legalist Philosophy

The formative years of the Chinese Empire, from 1200 BCE to 200 CE, were characterized by several key trends including: (1) the rapid growth and influence of Taoism, (2) an almost continual succession of hard-fought wars between states and emperors, (3) increasingly Legalist policies of some emperors, and (4) increasingly ruthless punishment of Taoists and other social or religious organizations that caused problems for the emperors and their rulership.

Maintaining power and tight control of the entire state was seemingly the emperors' most important objective, despite their treatment of the peasants, Sages, and philosophers.

As the common people began to honor and then deify the Taoist sages, they most likely began to show significantly greater respect for their teachers than for their royal families. Even if the emperors didn't see it themselves, their loyal advisors and military personnel would have undoubtably noticed these royal infractions and reported the incidents to the emperor's inner circle.

As the Taoist teachings became more renowned, many Chinese intellectuals also became Taoist followers. This, by itself, most likely also worried the ruling class. But even without the added influence of the growth in Taoism, the constant possibilities of new wars or revolts caused a natural increase in the strict priorities of the ruling class.

The Legalist Impact on the Tao Te Ching

The Tao Te Ching is a beautiful, inspirational book - written by several different authors.

According to most current scholars, it is a compilation of poems and quotes from the teachings of various ancient Chinese mystic philosophers including some of the ancient Taoists, Lao Tzu, several contemporary Zhou and Han Taoist sages, and Legalist philosophers.

Most scholars now believe that the Tao Te Ching was a compilation of different Taoist poems and statements from several different individuals.

There is considerable debate over the fictional or historical existence of Lao Tzu. If he did exist, Lao Tzu was only one of the many contributors to the Tao Te Ching.

Many modern scholars now believe that some of most outspoken Legalist philosophers, like Han Feizi, either heavily influenced the Tao Te Ching poems that discuss the relationship of the emperors to the people, or perhaps even wrote these poems themselves.

It is entirely possible that Han Feizi was actually the author of about thirty of the poems in the Tao Te Ching.

Similarly, many of the great Taoist doctrines that were created in the Zhou, Han, and Qin dynasties were also compilations.

Lao Tzu by Pascal Deloche

CHAPTER 4

THE AGE OF ENLIGHTENMENT

2000–200 BCE

The Yellow Emperor meets Taoist sage Guang Chengzi in 2698 BCE

The Tao Te Ching, by Lao Tzu and others, is published in 200 BCE

Most people, even some scholars, view Lao Tzu as the founder of Taoism, but that isn't true. The Tao Te Ching, published in approximately 200 BCE, should be viewed as the beginning of a religious path that has overshadowed the original Taoist consciousness path for the past two thousand years.

Today, direct (non-cognitive) consciousness paths are equally as popular as the Taoist religion. And the popularity of consciousness paths is strongly trending upward.

Key Spiritual Events in Ancient China

Age of Tribal Shamans	**8000–1121 BCE**
The Way to Heaven	8000 BCE
Yellow dragons	7000 BCE
Shaman I-Ching	4000 BCE
Age of Taoist Mystics	**5000–2000 BCE**
Jade Taoist tablets	5000 BCE
Taoist mysticism	5000–500 BCE
Tao consciousness	2000–150 BCE
Age of Emperors	**2698–200 BCE**
Yellow Emperor	2698–2598 BCE
Hsia dynasty	2205–1765 BCE
Shang dynasty	1766–1121 BCE
Chinese language	1200 BCE
Mandate of Heaven	1122 BCE
Zhou dynasty	1122–221 BCE
Age of Enlightenment	**2000–200 BCE**
Tai Shang Gan Ying Pian	600 BCE
100 Schools of Thought	500–221 BCE
Fang-Shih occultists	500 BCE–500 CE
Confucius I-Ching	551–479 BCE
Zhuangzi	450 BCE
Lao Tzu	450–350 BCE
Shang-Yang Legalism	350 BCE
Nei-Yeh	350 BCE
Extant Tao Te Ching	200 BCE
Age of Taoist Religion	**150 BCE–Now**
Han Dynasty	206 BCE–220 CE
Shrine of Lao Tzu	150 BCE

Shaman Influence on Chinese Culture

Since the beginning of the earliest civilizations in ancient China, shamans were highly respected for their magical powers, for their ability to talk to the gods, and for their spiritual wisdom. That sense of respect among Chinese people remained reasonably strong throughout the entire period of ancient China (8000–100 BCE) and through the entire period of the Han dynasty (206 BCE to 220 CE).

In the beginning their influence was primarily concentrated within their nomadic and settled tribes. Over time, as described in earlier chapters, many of their mystic visions enabled the Taoist mystics to create a new path focused on meditation on Celestial Awareness.

The shamanist doctrine, and the shamans' magical practices continued to grow even as the Taoist path continued to expand. Before the advent of the 100 Schools of Thought (500–221 BCE) the shaman path and the Taoist path dominated Chinese religious and spiritual activities.

Many members of the Shang and Zhou royal families depended on the predictions and the advice of shamans. During this same period Taoist sages heavenly influenced other Chinese emperors. For example, the Yellow Emperor heavily relied on the advice and Taoist teachings of Guang Chengzi. But all of the Shang emperors as well as the first Zhou dynasty emperor relied on the advice of their favorite shamans.

Over time, the shamans picked up and utilized several elements of the Taoist path. Over time, many shamans defended their influence by claiming that they too could help the emperors to learn how to become as godly and as immortal as the Taoist sages.

Shaman Yarrow Sticks

Tribal shamans were the first fortune tellers in ancient China.

As discussed by David Hinton in his recent translation and interpretation of the I Ching in his book *I Ching: The Book of Change*, told of two mythical dragons called Root-Breath and Lady She-Voice that emerged from Bright Prosperity Mountain. In this mythical legend, these two dragons were the mythical beings that created the entire cosmos. Root-Breath also created the hexagrams that were used by ancient shamans to predict the future.

Sometime before or during the Shang dynasty, a common practice of Chinese shamans was to throw bundles of yarrow sticks on the ground to predict the fortunes of both tribal peasants and dynasty emperors. The yarrow sticks were made from dried yarrow plants harvested in northern China.

An I-Ching Fortune Teller using Yarrow Sticks, 1914 photo by Elstner Hilton

As a living tribute to this ancient fortune-telling methodology and also as a modern tribute to e-commerce, you can still buy "ancient" yarrow sticks on websites like Amazon.com and Etsy.com.

The Yarrow Plant

A bundle of Yarrow Sticks on Amazon.com

The Shaman I-Ching

Eventually, the tribal shaman practice of using yarrow sticks for simple fortune-telling purposes led to the use of yarrow sticks to describe and predict cosmological and dynasty events.

As noted by David Hinton, Emperor Wen of the Zhou dynasty created the first formal definition of the I Ching divination system while imprisoned by the last emperor of the Shang dynasty. Years later, Emperor Wen's son, Emperor Wu, designated the I Ching as an important and official divination system of the Zhou dynasty.

During the 100 Schools of Thought, the Taoist doctrine was based on the meditative experiences of Taoist sages, and thus would have never used the I Ching as part of their doctrine. Nor was there ever any mention of the I Ching in the Tao Te Ching or in the Zhuangzi.

Unlike Lao Tzu, however, Confucius believed in the I Ching and often taught his students about the I Ching.

Almost a thousand years after the Emperor Wen, the Han dynasty deified Lao Tzu as a Taoist god, and created a new Taoist religion that also included the I Ching divination practice as a key element of the new Taoist religious doctrine.

The golden age of tribal shamanism lasted from about 5000 BCE to about 800 BCE. The succeeding golden age of "dynasty" shamanism was in play from roughly 800 BCE to 100 BCE. The golden years of Fang-Shih shamanism stretched from the Qin dynasty year of 221 BCE to the beginning of the Tang dynasty in 618 CE.

Some things have changed. Some things never change.

In our modern age most of the disciples and teachers of consciousness paths simply view the I Ching either as a Taoist-religion practice or as a fortune-telling method.

Modern-day Taoist religions often include the I Ching as part of their Taoist practice.

The Taoist Doctrine

The Taoist path originated in ancient China around 5000 BCE as a blend of shamanistic beliefs and a Tao consciousness set of meditation practices and beliefs. Accordingly, the jade tablets that were used to teach the initial Taoist path continually illustrated and emphasized the path of the yellow dragon and the magical ways to heavenly awareness by following that path.

Throughout the Shang and Western Zhou dynasties (1766–770 BCE), there was a massive increase in the manufacturing of jade Taoist tablets. The availability of these tablets contributed to make the Taoist teachings clearer and more popular. This led to a tremendous increase in the popularity and size of the Taoist path.

The other significant factor that emerged during this time was an increase in the number of new Taoist tablets that did not use yellow dragon symbolism.

There was, instead, a new emphasis on the heavenly Tao consciousness itself that is at the very core of human awareness — as illustrated by the empty circle in the center of every Taoist tablet.

Thus, the Taoist doctrine slowly shifted to an emphasis on consciousness meditation practices as the way to achieve *Jade Pure* Tao awareness (luminous, harmonic, clear awareness).

By the end of the Zhou dynasty in 221 BCE, the Taoist, Confucian, and Legalist philosophers rarely mentioned the original Path of the Yellow Dragons. But they frequently mentioned the Taoist path of inner training (meditation) on the vital essence (consciousness).

As evidenced by the Taoist publications (e.g., the Tai Shang Gan Ying Pian in 600 BCE, the Zuang Zi in 450 BCE, the Nei-Yeh in 350 BCE, and the Tao Te Ching in 250 BCE) that were created between about 600–200 BCE, the focus was on achieving Tao awareness by discovering and holding jing shen consciousness, discovering your vital essence, holding on to the One/Tao, effortlessly practicing wu wei Tao, or by practicing *Jade Pure* Tao awareness.

Taoist tablets decorated with yellow dragons were still being manufactured in the Qin and Han dynasties because of their cultural significance and their appeal to new spiritual seekers.

The Foundational Tao Scriptures

The five most important Taoist scriptures are the ancient Huang Long jade tablets, the Tai Shang Gan Ying Pian, the Zuangzi, the Nei-Yeh, and the Tao Te Ching.

These five priceless, cherished documents formed the foundation of the initial Taoist consciousness path and the subsequent Taoist religion.

Huang Long – 5000–50 BCE

As we've already seen, Huang Long, or the Path of the Yellow Dragon was the original Taoist path. Its basic emphasis on Tao consciousness, inner cultivation, and a wu wei lifestyle remained as the central Taoist doctrine in ancient China for over four thousand years.

A simple review of the thousands of jade Taoist tablets that were consistently carved from 5000 BCE to 50 BCE is clear evidence of the huge impact Huang Long had on every aspect of all following Taoist beliefs and practices. Furthermore, a precise comparison of these ancient teachings to the core mystic statements in all other key Taoist doctrines created in the Age of Enlightenment leads to the same conclusion.

The impact of Huang Long on both the Taoist doctrine and the various subsequent Taoist religions is thus far greater than the impact of any other Taoist teacher, path, or book.

Tai Shang Gan Ying Pian - 600 BCE

Tai Shang's treatise on Action and Response was first translated and interpreted by Li Shi Fu in 1964. The original text seems to have originated during the Spring and Autumn period of the Zhou dynasty (775–470 BCE). This ancient Taoist scripture bears the assumed author's name as Tai Shang. Li Shi Fu and some other scholars have claimed that it was most likely written by Lao Tzu, but based on the original date of the treatise, it would have been written before Lao Tzu was even born.

Although it is relatively unknown in the West, this is one of the most cherished books on Taoism in China. This short but precious book describes the heavenly nature of wu wei actions and responses that have a direct impact on both human life and on internal Tao consciousness.

Thus, the Gan Ying Pian points to the outward Taoist ways in which we should conduct our daily lives, and our attitudes toward the welfare of our worldwide family—as a complementary foundation to a meditational Taoist lifestyle of inward training.

It plainly states that a person who lives in a gracious and humble heart-mind state will benefit both that person and the entire worldwide community of people. Such a life, it hints, will help to establish one's divine inner nature (Tao), one's divine creativity, and one's divine perception (*Jade Pure* Celestial Awareness).

We should all passionately strive to live a gentle life revolving around an ongoing intention of establishing goodwill, and a divine inner nature. Once established, this will significantly contribute to "a community of common destiny for the human race" as honorably suggested by Xi Jin Ping.

The Zuangzi – 450 BCE

The Zuangzi was published somewhere between 450 and 350 BCE. Like the Gan Ying Pian, it heavily influenced the eventual author (s) of the Tao Te Ching. Also like the Gan Ying Pian, it is a seminal scripture that advises following a heartfelt, middle-way Taoist lifestyle of both inward and outward wu wei training.

By following Tao beyond all emotional and mental dualities, the Zuangzi suggests that we can all achieve true freedom, peace, and happiness in both life and death. We should thus practice a balanced path of inward and outward training, and *effortlessly hold on to Tao.*

Learn to let go of your petty emotions and your wayward thoughts. Ignore everything that simply comes and goes. Melt into Tao consciousness instead. The middle way to both personal and worldwide peace will magically appear right in front of you as gently float along in the divine river of Tao consciousness. The greatest achievements and inventions come easily – within Tao consciousness.

The Nei-Yeh – 350 BCE

The Nei-Yeh is an anonymous Taoist scripture, widely available approximately fifty years after the Zuangzi and at least one hundred years before the Tao Te Ching.

The Nei-Yeh scripture, like the ancient huang long tablets, was focused on the inward cultivation of Tao consciousness —through meditation and a mystic lifestyle.

Its emphasis is on discovering the Tao consciousness within you during your meditation practice — which results in a more passionate and loving nature in the outside world.

The Zuangzi and the Tai Shang Gan Ying Pian aim for the same result, but from opposite directions. These scriptures place a greater emphasis on becoming more Tao conscious and humble in the outside world — which results in a great ability to achieve inward progress as well.

The Nei-Yeh doctrine is similar to the medieval and consciousness traditions of Buddha's Tathagatta path, Advaita Vedanta, Zen Buddhism, Sri Ramana, and my Celestial Awareness path. Like all these similar paths, Nei-Yeh scripture describes the nature of enlightened consciousness and how to achieve it.

The Tao Te Ching – 250 BCE

As discussed in Chapter 3, the Tao Te Ching is a compilation of beautiful poems and sayings from several previous Taoist, Confucian, and Legalist philosophers.

Most of the poems are mystical gems that highlight the need and the value of holding on to Taoist virtues and to the natural, effortless, meditative lifestyle of Tao consciousness.

Additionally, one-third of the precious poems in the Tao Te Ching seem to be legalist statements extolling the virtues of Dynasty emperors that follow the same principles as the renowned Taoist monks.

Most true mystics view the Tao Te Ching as a beautiful transitional document that both describes the merit and the virtues of ancient Taoism and recognizes the potential for a new Taoist religious path in the emerging Chinese civilization.

The Popularity of Tao consciousness

The easiest way to describe the historical growth and decline of mystical Taoism is as follows:

(1) It originally evolved around 5000 BCE as a new, mystical path that used modified shaman tribal beliefs as an introduction to the Taoist path.

(2) Somewhere between 2000 BCE and 1000 BCE the emphasis shifted to a meditative inward training lifestyle and Tao consciousness.

(3) During the Zhou dynasty (1122–221 BCE), it grew to become one of the most important direct-consciousness spiritual lifestyles in ancient China.

(4) It heavily influenced the teachings of future shamanistic, philosophical, and religious organizations.

(5) It almost faded into obscurity by the end of the Qin dynasty in 207 BCE.

(6) It re-emerged and was redefined at the beginning of the Eastern Han dynasty in 21 CE as the new Taoist Religion.

All of the evolutionary achievements in Chinese language, art, culture, science, and manufacturing combined to foster the growth of the Taoist path unit that played a major role in Chinese philosophy and religion during the course of the Zhou dynasty.

The Eastern Zhou (771–221 BCE) phase of the Zhou dynasty is remembered by both historians and philosophers as the Golden Age of Chinese philosophy.

The emphasis of Tao consciousness began around 2000 BCE and lasted — as a golden age — until about 200 BCE. The renowned philosopher Mencius (372–280 BCE) named Taoism, along with Confucianism, and seven other paths as the predominant spiritual paths within China during that time frame.

However, the Legalist movement and its dominating influence in the Qin and Han dynasties, along with its resistance to organized religions, over time led to the destruction of a significant percentage of Taoist temples, sages, and books.

By the end of the Western Han dynasty in 8 CE, Taoism had almost faded into obscurity.

However, many new, and returning, Tao Sages have been born to teach different forms of Tao consciousness on Earth. For brief periods of time many of these new Tao consciousness paths have thrived.

And I'm one of those teachers who have returned to teach Tao consciousness once again!

Taoist temple on Wu Dang Mountain

Ancient Experiences in Tao Consciousness

The primary claim of Taoist teachers was that they could reach *Jade Pure Celestial Awareness* through a lifelong spiritual devotion to the flow of Tao consciousness.

During the golden age of Tao consciousness, countless other stories emerged of sensational Taoist sages who had been reincarnated many times, over thousands of years, to teach Taoism in ancient China. The legend of Guang Chengzi and the Yellow Emperor was just one of many such stories.

There were also numerous stories of Taoist immortals who were not only reincarnated, but who could also occasionally disappear into thin air and reappear hours later during their meditation practices.

These inner experiences of ancient fully enlightened Taoist mystics are very real. From both personal experience and from a careful examination of the Taoist tablets, it's clear to me that even in the early days of the Chinese dynasties, many of the Taoist sages had the following types of experiences:

(1) watching their body physically disappear as they continued to meditate on the Tao;

(2) real-time multidimensional consciousness;

(3) a cosmic consciousness that interconnects, and constantly nurtures, millions of other conscious beings;

(4) co-creating the Cosmos within Jade Pure awareness;

(5) staying within Tao consciousness as that consciousness creates new forms of energy, molecules, objects, sentient beings, and planets; and

(6) remembering dozens of past lives.

Reincarnation

The concept of reincarnation over time may seem impossible to many people, but it's evident to highly enlightened mystics. Deep within, on the way to divine awareness, every mystic can see, and even experience, previous and future lifetimes.

My first visions of previous reincarnations came as a young teenager, just after my initial meditation on the floating Tao disk. Over the next 12 months I traveled back and forth in time; and experienced many past lives in Atlantis, in the Mideast, and in China. Later, in the Taipei Historical Museum in 1994, I had an immediate download of the entire ancient Taoist doctrine that I had previously taught in ancient China. The mere fact of being able to remember these ancient teachings so clearly is an obvious verification of the value and the importance of reincarnation to mystics.

Guang Chengzi most likely said something similar to the Yellow Emperor.

Taoist Immortals

If you've ever wondered why many of the greatest Taoist sages were referred to as immortal, just think about what it must have been like for a Chinese peasant to watch his Taoist sage physically disappear and then reappear minutes or hours later.

After having watched that type of experience, would there be any doubt about his sage's ability to leave the Earthly realm as he/she flew up through the mist and into the highest heavenly realms?

No. There would be any doubt at all. The peasant would have been immediately regarded the Taoist teacher as a "Heavenly Immortal" with the capability to fly in an invisible spirit form, much like the fabled yellow dragons that could also fly from Earth and up into the heavenly realms whenever they needed to.

Most university textbooks will probably say that the historical myths came first, but an enlightened mystic will always remind us to "go inside and experience the truth yourself – the truth about your own original nature as the heavenly creator of everything in existence."

As discussed in the next chapter, I also learned how to physically disappear and then reappear during a meditation session. For me, there's no mystery at all. It simply happens every now and then.

Mystical Tao consciousness is, by itself, a profound, celestial, wisdom teaching. However, to fully understand Tao consciousness as an integral part of Chinese culture and philosophy, we need to look at things from a much broader perspective.

From Mysticism to Religion

Most great religions that are familiar to us today started as small mystic paths of fewer than several dozen followers. Gradually, after the passing of several hundred years to half a millennia, they grew into formalized religions of hundreds of thousands, or even millions, of disciples.

Mystic teachers don't generally teach mental practices, prayers, mantra-repetition, or mind-body yoga to serious students that are seeking enlightenment. These types of cultivation practices are great tools for new seekers that want to lead a more spiritually minded lifestyle. And most mystics are happy to teach these methods to new spiritually minded seekers. But they also teach different mystic cultivation methods to their more advanced students.

Students that are drawn inward toward soul-conscious experiences, as well as old souls who are starting to experience mystical miracles, need cultivation methods and mystic teachings that enable and empower transpersonal experiences (e.g., beyond mind-body and time-space awareness).

Therefore, most mystic teachers, train their advanced students how to become "silently and effortlessly aware" of the celestial/divine consciousness (aka: direct awareness, *Jade Pure* Tao, immortal consciousness, soul consciousness, mystic enlightenment, etc.) within them. The true mystic paths are thus built around mystic meditation practices and real-time, non-cognitive, experiences of divine awareness. Their disciples usually have a subtle sense of the divine presence as well as a growing, or strong, "urge to merge" into divine consciousness.

CHAPTER 5

MEMOIRS OF A TAOIST SAGE

Me, in the Canadian Rocky Mountains

I'm not a guru with a turban or a high priest of an exalted religion. I'm just a simple man with warts and wrinkles and a lifetime of simple pleasures and hard work. And I'm an experienced teacher of mystic Taoism.

I've been to college, but I'm not a Ph.D. level scholar. I'm also not a trained archaeologist, a peer-reviewed philosopher, a renowned historian or a certified expert in languages and translations.

I'm just an old mystic, nearing the final phases of a mostly ordinary life. I was brought up in a middle-class home. I was a Cub Scout, and then a Boy Scout and then a Civil Air Patrol teenager. I worked full time in factories in high school and in college.

As a teenager, I didn't even know what Taoism was. I never read about it. Nor did I ever meet anyone who ever mentioned the word Taoism — until more than 10 years after I started meditating on Tao consciousness as a teenager.

During those ten years, I inwardly, and intuitively, lived and followed an intense wu wei, Taoist lifestyle — floating in a *Jade Pure* state of consciousness and meditating for several hours every day.

I'm grateful to be alive in such remarkable times, and to be able to discuss ancient Taoism with you. It's not a path that I chose, but it is the path that brought me to you. I thank all of you, everyone who is reading, or thinking about, this book for giving me the opportunity to follow the Taoist path with you.

In a very real sense, it is you who have drawn me into this life and through this Taoist path, and I thank you from the bottom of my heart.

What follows is a short description of the highlights and struggles of my simple life. It's my hope that it will illuminate the fact that anyone, living anywhere in this modern world, can follow the Taoist path to Celestial Awareness.

In this section, I will talk about a few of the miracles that I encountered. In later sections of this book, as we further explore the mystical Taoist teachings, I will describe additional miracles to help you understand what celestially enlightened mystics experience and understand.

Most of the people I've met in this life have assumed that I live a normal life. Most of my relatives as well as my friends and business associates have never suspected that I was often floating through the world in a magical, mystical state of intensely clear awareness.

However, my life has been ordinary in many ways, but my secret Taoist lifestyle has been very different indeed.

I've lived a quiet life, and to the best of my ability I've kept my mystic experiences secret — while pretending to be "normal." It didn't always work out that way, but I did my best to lead a private life as a mystic Taoist.

Wu Wei — All the Way

I was born in America in a hard-working, middle-class family of French Catholics. In fact, my father was a Catholic lay priest who worked full time in an automobile factory. He graduated from seminary college, but because of the death of his mother he was never able to become fully ordained.

In other words, he could live a married life and he could give the Sunday sermons, but he could not hear confessions or bless and distribute the Christian sacraments. He tried to raise me to become a priest as well, but that was simply not my destiny. I was not born to become a priest.

Unlike most infants that are born in the second trimester, I was born in the very first molecule of the womb. Moreover, I was fully awake in this molecule.

According to an analysis of the ancient Taoist tablets, many celestially enlightened Taoist sages were also awake, in *Jade Pure* Tao consciousness before the fetus even began to form.

I'll discuss this in greater detail in Chapter 8, but the following Taoist tablet was used to teach new seekers that Taoist saints were *Jade Pure* Tao conscious in the womb.

Floating in a stream of *Jade Pure* enlightened consciousness, I was able concentrate on Tao awareness while ignoring the energy patterns that were passing by my molecular form. I was simply holding on to the Tao during my meditation in the womb.

While silent, I floated through a sequence of various changes in my consciousness. But the most amazing change occurred in the first bubble/field of awareness.

My initial consciousness began to become less dense – just before it split into two additional bubbles of consciousness. This was my first experience of multidimensional awareness in this lifetime. I was fully aware within each bubble of awareness and aware of the same full awareness in the other two bubbles as well. The transformation into three bubbles was then followed by a multidimensional awareness in seven bubbles. My consciousness then transformed into fifteen bubbles, and so on, until the form of my new fetus began to take shape.

It's obvious to me that this life that we lead, over time, will eventually tell us everything we need to know, if we stay passionately curious and intimately involved in the transformations that occur.

As this birthing process continued, I simultaneously remembered and relived the same type of process that occurred at the genesis of my soul and at the birth of the cosmos. This was a deep Taoist secret that I kept to myself for the first seventy years of my life.

As we shall see when we explore the Taoist tablets in Chapter 8, many of the great, ancient Taoist, mystics had these same types of experiences in the womb.

Like many children, I floated in and out of pure awareness – usually aware of nothing except enlightened awareness – for the first few years. My Catholic parents were frightened from the very beginning. Apparently, when I was just an infant, fire trucks and teddy bears used to materialize above my head, floating and following me as I crawled around the house.

My dear mother thought I must be possessed by the devil and wanted the Catholic church to send an exorcist to cure me. My dad was frightened too, but he was apparently more concerned about protecting his role as a Catholic lay priest.

On hundreds of occasions, they scolded me, angrily warning me not to talk about my mystic experiences.

Moreover, I overheard their arguments over what to do about me dozens of times, during the day and especially late at night. My father won all the arguments, which lasted on and off for another fifteen years.

When their friends or relatives came over, they simply agreed to send me to my bedroom. Fortunately, it was convenient for them, and it was an ideal opportunity for me to secretly melt back into delightful streams of pure Tao awareness. To most other people, I was simply another ordinary child.

Here I am in a Cub Scout uniform, with a baseball glove – at 9 years old.

Schoolwork was very easy for me. I got high marks, and skipped two full years of school. In junior high, I had the ability to read three pages a minute in combination with photographic memory. In a lot of my tests, I never read the questions or the multiple-choice answers. In a wu wei state, I simply put down the correct answers – they came to me automatically. Even after I began working full time in the tenth grade, I still did well in school.

I was called a math prodigy, but I was just floating through life as a silent observer – deeply immersed within celestial Tao awareness. Everything else was happening automatically including the artificial intelligence functions of the mind. For example, in high school calculus tests I started and finished my one-hour tests in about fifteen minutes. My math professor thought at first that I was cheating, because several of my hypotheses were at a PhD level. But I was just writing down the formulas that were flowing through me.

When he discovered that I wasn't cheating, he was shocked. I was simply intrigued by his reaction. Wasn't everyone just like me? I was beginning to see that they weren't. I was obviously the same as everyone else in many external ways, but much different internally.

Although I didn't know it at the time, I was practicing an advanced stage of Wu wei.

In some ways my life seemed easy, but it was also filled with a lot of hard work and tough challenges.

In the last two years of high school, I started working full time. I would wake up, have some breakfast, and then walk to school at 7:00, finishing my classes around 3:30 p.m.

After that, I'd drop my books off at home, grab a sandwich, and then go to work.

I worked in a distribution warehouse for one year, and full time in railroad and/or automobile factories for the next five years (two years of high school and three years of college). I'd get home from the factory around 1:00 a.m., sleep for about three hours, get up, do an hour of homework, and then start a new day again. Rinse and repeat - mostly in a state of clear awareness.

It was a tough life. I'd often come home, totally exhausted, in the middle of the night, covered in grease and industrial dirt. There was little time to sit for meditation. Fortunately, however, I could stay in a clear, meditative awareness throughout most of the day.

Most true mystics are honest about the fact that humans have karma, and because of their karma they simply cannot maintain clear awareness throughout the entire day. But the clear Tao awareness is always there when you need it.

Fortunately, the ability to meditate while I was working and attending classes made life not only easier but more enjoyable. When you're in a bubble of *Jade Pure* clear Tao awareness, you're also in a bubble of bliss.

For an ancient Chinese, peasant, farmer or factory worker, the Taoist Way to Heaven meditation would have had a similar joyful effect. Even then, three thousand or more years ago, a life of hard labor in an often-brutal world would have been much easier if you knew that you had a chance to eventually abide in the heavenly realms.

In 1965, when I took the four-hour national Scholastic Aptitude Test in high school, I finished it in about forty-five minutes.

The SAT is a tough required entrance exam for high school students who want to qualify to attend US and Canadian colleges and universities. It is a test in writing, mathematics, and logic with hundreds of questions. Most students can't complete it because of its length.

I answered all the questions and had only seven wrong answers. This isn't possible to accomplish if you're carefully reading every question. But I didn't have to read the questions or even the multiple-choice answers. In a stream of clear awareness, I simply wrote down the correct answer and moved on. The correct *glowing* alphabetical letter usually appeared, floating just above the test in front of me.

This same type of miracle has occurred many different times throughout my life. And I've met four other individuals who had a similar experience on the SAT.

This is a normal lifestyle for anyone who has reached the third or fourth stage of wu wei. *You literally can live in this world without being of it!*

During my high school years, I also became increasingly more psychic — with many new abilities like reading minds and seeing things before they would happen. I didn't really know what was going on in my life. I just knew that I was different, but I didn't yet know why.

And then one day, I had an astonishing experience — something that forever changed the direction and purpose of my life.

My First Discovery of Taoist Tablets

Over sixty years ago, as a twelve-year-old boy, before I had even heard or read about meditation, I intuitively sat down one day to meditate and began to melt deeply into a state of clear awareness. Suddenly I saw a vision of a green disk floating in the air directly in front of me.

It looked like the green disk in this photo.

As a teenager, I was absolutely clueless. What was this disk, and why was it just floating in front of me?

It looked like a green vinyl 78-rpm record with a hole in the middle. But I had never seen a green record. Then this mysterious disk started floating toward my head.

I patiently watched as it floated seemingly effortlessly into my head — into my eye center. The eye center is in your forehead, just above and behind your eyes.

After that happened, I could travel back and forth though millions of years of past and future lifetimes.

Without knowing it, I had discovered one of the magical properties of the mystical Taoist tablets.

Hundreds of Ancient Tablets

About thirty years after that disk meditation, I went to Taiwan as a high-tech computer executive. I was hired by the Taiwanese government as the leading outside architect of their business plan for a new microcomputer industry.

I traveled back and forth to Taiwan for about three years, training thousands of new and current high-tech companies, executives, and engineers on designing, building, and marketing microcomputer products.

During one of my free weekends in Taipei, I went to a large, beautiful jade exhibit at the Historical Museum. And as I rounded a corner to view a new display, I came face-to-face with the same jade disk that I had seen, as a teenager, in my first meditation experience thirty years earlier.

Even more amazing was the fact that this five-thousand-year-old jade tablet was the same sacred disk I used for my meditation – when I'd taught Taoism in ancient China.

I knew every scratch, the color of every vein, and every other detail. This was the same meditation tablet that had helped me to travel the Taoist Way to Heaven and to achieve *Jade Pure* awareness.

I fell to my knees as my old memories of the entire ancient Taoist teachings flooded, or "downloaded" back into me - in just a few seconds. I knew then what I was born to do. I'd been born once again to teach the mystic path of ancient Taoism.

As I stared at my five-thousand-year-old meditation stone, I also became aware that I wasn't meant to start teaching again until many years later. I realized it would not be proper until I was an old man, fully enlightened, and retired from my technical career before starting to teach Taoism consciousness again.

I thus spent a good part of the next few decades following the Taoist path of clear awareness, writing down the teachings and finding additional drawings and pictures of age-old Taoist tablets. Over the past years, I've found over one hundred new renderings of additional Taoist tablets.

I'm now seventy-four years old, and this book represents the starting point of my new Taoist teachings about Celestial Awareness.

Other Incredible Miracles

My entire life has been a parade of miracles that simply happened automatically. They happened when either I needed that miracle to happen, or the world needed that miracle to happen. But throughout it all, I've simply been a spectator.

A lot of gurus *claim* that they create thousands of miracles in their lives, but that's not how it really happens. Most miracles simply happen automatically, without any intention, imagination or effort.

Moreover, when a disciple of an advanced guru/teacher experiences a miracle, it is usually created automatically by the accumulated merit of that disciple's own past experiences. Miracles happen to both reward and guide the disciple forward on his/her path. False gurus often try to falsely take credit for the miracles that happen to their disciples, but they shouldn't.

Gifted, spiritual teachers aren't born just to create miracles. They're usually born to fulfill a specific role on Earth. But all advanced souls usually experience more miracles than ordinary people, and highly advanced sages usually experience thousands of miracles during their lifetime.

My Near-Death Experience

On March 21, 1969, the day of the spring equinox, I was sitting in a lounge at Eastern Michigan University meditating with some of my friends. Suddenly, my inner consciousness rose up and I opened my eyes to see my friends flinching nervously as a huge rainstorm began.

Instinctively, I walked toward the exit door, and they all followed me. I opened the door and witnessed a tremendous storm with countless fat raindrops exploding as they hit the ground. I walked into the rain and my friends followed, some next to me and others right behind me. My instincts caused me to look into the sky in the opposite direction of the sun, which was still visible through the rain.

Just then, I saw a vision of Death — a large skeleton in a black robe, holding the scythe and staring directly into my eyes. He was so tall that his head was higher than the nearby clouds.

A drawing by Dante Corvus

I could see him, but none of my companions could. So I turned to them and softly said, "This is the year that I die. I have to go on alone to prepare for my death. And you need to leave me. Go find your own path and have a wonderful life."

A few hours later, after the storm had passed, I saw a god-like figure in the sky. As it looked at me, my consciousness grew by leaps and bounds. And I said to myself, "Maybe this isn't the year that I die after all."

About two weeks later, I was walking down a sidewalk in Ann Arbor, Michigan, when a golden ball of light appeared in the air about five feet in front of me. An angel-like creature stepped out of the ball of light, placed his right hand on my left shoulder, and said, "The gods are very happy with you. Go forward." Then the angel stepped backward into the ball of light and disappeared.

Another two weeks passed, and the same thing happened again in another town and on a different sidewalk. It was just a slightly different angel.

Two further weeks went by, and the same event happened the same way yet on a different sidewalk in a different town. And it was a different angel.

About another month after that, I awoke one morning with a vivid vision of my impending death. I saw myself driving down a city street in Detroit, lined with tall green lampposts. As I was driving along, a large pink Cadillac appeared suddenly out of a side street on my right. The driver obviously didn't see me, and a few seconds later he ran right straight into the side of my tiny Volkswagen.

I remember this vision very clearly, even though it happened more than fifty years ago. I was thrown out my car door window headfirst and into a tall green iron lamppost. Seconds later, I was floating in a spirit form above my dead body, as a small fountain of blood was still streaming out of my head. And then I started floating up into the astral zone passing hundreds of planets in dozens of different regions. Eventually, I came to a black empty stretch of deep space. But it wasn't just empty space; it was a region of divine consciousness.

And then the vision ended.

One morning a month later, I woke up and everything felt as light as a feather. There was a strong spiritual energy in the air. I immediately knew that this was the day. This was the day that I was meant to die.

And in that moment, I fully understood what the angels meant. Yes, I was meant to die. This was also my test of faith. All three angels had told me to go forward – even if I was meant to die. Buddha was tested under the Bodhi tree. Yeshua and many other saints had been previously tested, as I was about to be tested, at the point of death.

I just smiled. This was such a beautiful drama. Such a beautiful dream. I took a shower, got dressed, and had a simple breakfast. And then I simply waited for my fate to come to me.

Wu wei is about letting the transient things and events in your life simply come and go, while you maintain your focus on the Celestial Awareness within you that never comes and goes. Celestial Awareness is the only thing in life that never comes and goes.

Thoughts and emotions come and go. Your cars and your houses come and go. Furniture and clothes come and go. Money and wealth come and go. Karma comes and goes. Friends and family come and go. Even your human life comes and goes.

But your clear awareness remains eternal.

About thirty minutes after breakfast, a friend called and asked whether I could come and pick up him and his girlfriend and then drive them to downtown Detroit. Ahh. It's such a beautiful gift to see your fate. To see the short cycles and long cycles as well. This was just another test.

"Sure, I'd be happy to," I said, and I picked them up and started driving. I said, "I don't know this area very well, so just be my navigator. Pick the streets that you want to drive on." About twenty minutes later, we were driving down the same street I had seen in my vision. This was the street on which I would die.

About ten minutes later I saw the pink Cadillac about fifty yards away from me. It was the car that would kill me.

I had plenty of time to stop and park my Volkswagen. I could have also slowed down or honked my horn to avoid the accident. But the angels had said to just go forward, so that's what I did. I went forward.

At that moment I noticed that my driver's-side car window was rolled down instead of up as it had in my vision. So, I rolled it up. Then I looked up. The Cadillac was coming straight toward me. I was in front of it, but the driver, apparently, could not see me.

This accident was meant to happen. And seconds later, it did.

Everything happened exactly the way it had played out in my previous vision. I was thrown through my driver's-side window, flying through the air, like a missile on track to hit its target. And when I hit the lamppost, it cracked my skull. Seconds later, I was floating above my body while the blood poured out of my head. I was dead, but fully conscious.

After that I floated up through the astral zones toward the region of deep space, exactly as I had in my vision. But it was so much more than just deep space; it was a heavenly region of divine awareness. It was the region of space that the Buddhists call *Mahakala*. I was still conscious as my awareness began to melt into and become this consciousness.

Over twenty years later, when the Karmapa of the Kagyu (one of the four major schools of Tibetan Buddhism) lineage met me, he immediately addressed me as Mahakala. I'm not Mahakala, I'm just a simple teacher. But many Buddhists have seen his energy within me.

It seemed as if I was only in the Mahakala region for a few moments, but two and half hours later, I awoke floating in a mist-like spirit form staring down at my dead body on an operating table in a hospital. There were about four people in the room and three of them were watching the head surgeon demonstrate his renowned golf putting stroke. A trickle of blood dripped down from the head of my dead body. Finally, one of the other surgeons said, "Well, let's stitch him up and send him down to the morgue.

Instinctively, I dove into the body, at the navel, opened my eyes and said, "Can I watch?" The surgeon right next to me dropped his scalpel and some other surgical device. I can still hear that scalpel bouncing on the floor. They quickly gassed me, and I woke up hours later with an enormous headache. I had been declared dead for two and a half hours before they stitched me back up.

From that point onward, I was different in two important ways. First, I had no fear of death. Second, my power to concentrate on the source of my awareness, and my totality of consciousness, was significantly enhanced.

The Programmers Test at General Motors

About six months later, without any experience in computer programming, and without a bachelor's degree, I answered a job advertisement for an entry-level computer programmer job at General Motors. The ad had required a bachelor's degree in either accounting or mathematics.

I didn't meet the requirements, but I went in for the programmer test anyway. It was supposed to be a two-hour test, but I finished it in less than thirty minutes. The supervisor asked me if I'd had a problem with the test. I said no, and after looking at my resume, he said, "Well, it's Friday afternoon, so why don't I just check your answers quickly so you can go home early?" I said, "Sure, why not?"

About twenty minutes later he came back in a mild state of shock. I hadn't made a single mistake. He then said, stammering, "I don't know how to grade you. Your test was perfect, but you have more bonus points than I can even use!" I softly said, "Can I have the job?" He agreed, and that was how I started my career in the computer industry.

The Speech at the Radha Soami Meeting

About six months later, I attended a Radha Soami meeting in downtown Detroit. Radha Soami is a spiritually minded group founded in India in 1861. The regional secretary of that group had asked me to give a speech that day.

I wasn't prepared and I really didn't understand the Radha Soami faith very well at that time. As he announced me, I bowed my head, and gave away my awareness to the Divine. Seconds later, I lifted my head up, only to discover that I was now standing at the speaker's podium and answering questions about the speech that I had apparently given.

That was the first time I fully realized that when you're in a state of clear awareness, your mind and body (1) are outside of your awareness, and (2) will act perfectly for you in the outside world.

None of these contemporary saints had any previous knowledge of me, or knew that I was planning to write a book.

I gave keynote speeches at Intel on semiconductor design, to a group of quantum physicists on the creation of the universe, to the American Medical Association on the future of computers in the surgery room, to the Federal Treasury and the International Monetary Fund on long-range econometrics, and to the United Nations on the fifty-year future gross national product (GNP) of the top three hundred countries. I was giving keynote speeches on complex subjects that I often didn't understand at all.

I was in an advanced state of wu wei consciousness, and I just floated through the speeches.

The Invention of the Spreadsheet

In 1972 I went to work at Mohawk Data Sciences as an entry-level minicomputer programmer. One Monday morning, a salesman named Roger Smith asked me if I could spend the week creating a simple program for the welfare department for the state of Michigan. Since my week was reasonably clear, I agreed, and I asked, "what type of computer do I need to write this program for?" He said, "The 2300." I wasn't familiar with that machine, so I asked him what it was. He replied, rather tentatively, "I don't know. It's in Tom's office, next door to your office. Ask him."

So, I walked into Tom's office and explained to him what Roger wanted me to do. Tom said, "That's impossible. Turn around - it's in that crate. But it's a prototype, right off the factory floor. It's just for show-and-tell right now. It doesn't have program compilers yet. Tell him you can't do it."

But my wu wei intuition was telling me something different. It was telling me to move ahead. So, I said, "No problem. I can write it in machine code language" - even though I had never written any program at the machine code level. Tom then sternly replied, "Greg, tell him NO! The 2300 doesn't even have an operating system, or a machine code language yet." I said, "Thanks, Tom. I'll take care of it," and I walked out of the room.

Roger was standing there waiting for me. You might guess what he said and how I responded. He said, "Can you do it?" And I said "Sure. No problem." After all, I was floating in a stream of bright white Tao consciousness.

So, I entered my tiny office, and closed and locked the door. After calling Eastern Airlines to book a ticket to Chicago, where I could compile a program, I sat at my desk, put the manila folder with the job request on top of my desk, turned off the lights, and began to meditate.

Roughly eight hours later, I opened my eyes and noticed a three-foot-long green metal tray on my desk almost filled with punched cards. My office door was still locked from the inside and there were no punch card machines in the building. The tray of punched cards had clearly been automatically manifested out of thin air by divine awareness.

(In those days, you had to keypunch your program statements into the punch cards, then instruct a minicomputer to read the cards to create an object file that another computer could use to run a program.)

There was also an eighty-page document on my desk defining a new MINQ (multiple enquiry) operating system for the 2300 microcomputer that I had somehow magically designed – while I was meditating in the dark in a locked office.

No big deal. I went home and had a nice dinner with my family. The next day, after having meditated for over eight hours, there was a second tray of punched cards and another typed document describing the invention of a new machine code programming language for the 2300 microcomputer. By the way, this was the very first microcomputer that was ever built.

The third day brought the same routine, and the same type of result. The second tray was now filled with punched cards, and there was a new typed and stapled document describing the invention of the microcomputer spreadsheet.

I packed everything up and flew to the Chicago computer center the same day. In the evening I had a perfect compile on the first try. This was extremely rare in the early 1970s. A perfect compile for a new operating system, by itself, usually took at least six months to achieve. I had one hour, and my wu wei compile was just fine. I knew exactly what I was doing when I threw away the punched cards and then went to my hotel room in Chicago. The next day, Thursday, I caught an afternoon flight to Lansing, Michigan.

When I got to my hotel room in Lansing, a welfare department manager called me to explain that the schedule had changed. He needed me to give a presentation to the top welfare department managers about this software that I was scheduled to install on Friday. I said, "No problem, but I need to stop by your office tonight to make some new transparencies and copies of my presentation for the meeting." He said, "Sure, I'll call the night guard and have him set things up for you."

At this point, I still didn't have any slides to print, and I still didn't know any details about the program I had created. But I was floating in a wu wei stream of clear awareness, and I didn't have a worry in the world.

I got to the new building, found an office that I could lock from the inside, sat down to meditate, and in the early morning hours I finally opened my eyes. There was a stack of thirty typed presentations for me to hand out to the welfare department managers and a new stack of black-and-white transparencies.

I drove back to the hotel, took a shower, shaved, put on a suit, and then drove over to the welfare department. After I gave a great presentation, I installed the program on a new 2300 that had just arrived at the office. Without blinking, I fired up the computer, and the new MINQ spreadsheet application worked flawlessly. Over the next two years, there was never a single problem with that application. I had left Mohawk Data Sciences by then, and the customer eventually went on to purchase a new computer.

Throughout my career in the computer industry, there were at least twenty similar occurrences. During my career, I also invented presentation-graphics, the first pro forma for PCs, the smartphone, and several other really cool inventions.

These inventions were things that the world needed, and I was happy to be able to help in any way I could. I didn't think of myself as the real inventor. All these inventions happened automatically, while I was meditating in a Tao-like state of *Jade Pure* clear awareness.

One Last Thing

In 1975, at the Radha Soami ashram in India, Huzar Charan Singh, a Radha Soami saint pulled me out of a crowd of over 250,000 Radha Soami disciples to ask me what my meditation practice was – while everyone else was patiently and eagerly waiting for Charan Singh to give the daily *satsang* (sermon).

Earlier in 1971, after going so deep inside clear awareness that I could experience Charan Singh's own meditation practice, I realized that it was the same Tao consciousness practice that I'd been practicing since my teenage years. So I instinctively dropped the official Radha Soami audible life stream practice in 1971 and switched back to the Taoist practice of direct-Celestial-Awareness.

When I explained this to Charan Singh, he said, "Wonderful. You've found the perfect path. The path of all great mystics. Don't do anything else. Just keep practicing this method. One day it will take you to Sach Kand (heavenly consciousness). Also, Radha Soami is about to become a religion. When it does, you need to leave to discover, follow, and understand other mystic paths. Then, you need to start teaching and writing books about this perfect path." Several days later, in his rose garden meeting, he told me in front of about forty other disciples that "someday, in this life, you will also reach Sach Kand."

And during the next ten years, several other highly advanced mystics and saints said something similar. When I met Amma, the hugging saint, for the first time, she hugged me and whispered, "You have to write that book." When I sent a copy of my initial proposed summary of this book to Nan Huai-chin, a Buddhist saint living in China (1918–2012), he wrote to me and said: "You have to write that book."

When I first met Shamar Rimpoche, the co-leader of the Kagyu lineage he immediately said, "You have to write that book." When I met the Karmapa of the Kagyu lineage for the second time, he immediately said, "You have to write that book." When I met Ananda Ma for the first time, she said: "You have to write that book." When I met one of the other Rimpoches who had taught the Dalai Lama, he automatically said, "Oh my. Your mind is perfectly clear. You have to write that book." When I met Sai Ma for the first time, she quickly said, "You have to write that book."

None of these contemporary saints had any previous knowledge of me, or that I was planning to write a book. In the first few seconds after meeting me, however, they all independently said the same thing: "You have to write that book."

When I traveled to India in October 2018 to meet Captain Ji, an Indian saint who was Nirvana-conscious, he said, "My guru, Faqir Ji, who died years ago, physically manifested in front of me last night and said that today was an historical day in spiritual history, for I would meet the man who is going to write the book that will help to launch the next Golden Age. And here you are. You have to write that book."

And so, I'm here with you now as an old, poor, and simple man, who is compelled to write this book.

This is the book you are reading right now. I'm writing it for you and for every soul who eventually reads it. I'm writing this book to enlighten the path to Celestial Awareness.

CHAPTER 6

THE AGE OF MODERN TAOISM

Tao Consciousness

Modern-day celestial mystics like me, Sri Ramana, and Maharaj Nisargadatta have a clear understanding of mystic *consciousness*, including what it means today and what it meant in ancient times.

Mysticism consciousness is an ancient wisdom that is impossible to grasp because it *can't* be grasped. It's also a myriad of astonishing, precious, soulful experiences that are difficult to explain, even after you initially discover them.

But I have begun teaching these same ancient lessons again.

Mysticism is hard to see because consciousness is something that does not depend on, or even make use of, your physical eyesight.

Mystic consciousness is also hard to think about because Taoist Celestial Awareness experiences do not happen in the mind, or even in the brain.

Likewise, you cannot listen to the celestial sounds of different mystic regions because experiences of Celestial Awareness immediately disappear when you try to mentally (cognitively) listen, see, feel, or memorize a mystic experience.

Similarly, dreams or trances caused by shamanistic practices, and herbal or chemical hallucinogens (e.g., LSD, ayahuasca, marijuana, opium, etc.) happen in the mind and thus are not mystic experiences of Tao consciousness.

Even astral experiences are not considered by advanced mystics to be clear awareness experience of the soul. Astral experiences simply happen when an individual develops the capability of having mental experiences in other dimensions. Astral experiences happen just before and just after you leave an enlightened, soulful experience in non-cognitive clear awareness. Astral experiences can also be triggered by near-death experiences or simply by everyday synchronicities.

Mystic experiences of clear awareness happen only when you are completely beyond mind-body and space-time awareness.

Enlightened clear awareness and mind-body awareness are mutually exclusive. If you are using the mind, you cannot have a mystical Taoist experience at the same time.

Mystic practices of clear awareness don't start with physical, or mental yoga practices like hatha (breath) yoga, kundalini (energy) yoga, mantra yoga, or sound-current yoga. These types of spiritual practices keep you in the mind.

True mystic meditation in clear awareness can't truly be called a practice. Mystic meditation doesn't require any effort. Just as it happened five thousand years ago in ancient China and in numerous spiritual retreats in contemporary times, mystic clear awareness meditation starts with effortlessly melting into timeless experiences of intensely clear, vibrant awareness that mysteriously arises from within you.

When true Taoist enlightenment happens, a mystic person experiences states of clear awareness, freedom, peace, luminosity, and joy that are at least ten times greater than anything that they would experience while they were in their mind. As one goes even deeper into higher levels of Taoist clear awareness, these differences between fragmented mind-body awareness and mystically clear awareness become significantly greater.

In the highest, or heavenly, levels of clear, Celestial Awareness, every new experience that you have in the future within lower levels of physical, mental, and astral planes can also be experienced within your real-time, mystically clear awareness.

It occurs this way because everything within the entire cosmos is also within the same celestial, divine, consciousness.

Scholars versus Mystics

In a quest to understand the true meaning of ancient Taoism, it's also crucial to understand the key differences between scholars and mystics. ***Scholars and mystics are equally precious and important.*** However, they see things from vastly different perspectives, and thus, they describe things much differently.

When talking about scholars, I'm referring to a variety of passionately curious people, their knowledge and the expression of that knowledge. This includes historians, philosophers, religious scholars, sinologists, archaeologists, and poets.

Scholars read books to discover the outer knowledge about things, and mystics effortlessly meditate on clear awareness to discover the inner nature of things.

Likewise, scientists experiment to see how physical things work or to see how they were physically created. Mystics enter creative Tao awareness to experience how consciousness creates the ten thousand things.

Scholars write books to describe additional details and theories about their point of view. Mystics write books that help to eliminate the mind-body confusion that obstructs the clear Tao awareness that is beyond all points of view.

How Scholars Treat Mystical Writings

When you read a book about ancient Taoism, or any other mystical text (e.g., the Vedas, the Jap Ji, the Tao Te Ching, etc.), it is very important to understand *how* scholars, historians, and philosophers have interpreted the pictograms, poems, and prose created by the ancient mystics in your book.

Of the several hundred books written about ancient Taoism by poets, scholars, archaeologists, historians, philosophers, and religious leaders, most likely only a very small number of these were written by highly enlightened mystics.

That's a big problem if you want to understand what the ancient mystics and Taoist sages were actually talking about.

Most authors of books on ancient Taoism are undoubtedly sincere and well read, but they often lack enough mystical experience in Celestial Awareness to properly recognize and discuss the in-depth wisdom of ancient Taoist sages.

Most scholars of Taoist literature spend at least eight years in prominent colleges and universities before they begin to write and publish books and essays on Taoism.

In comparison, most fully enlightened mystics spend at least forty years in intensive meditation before reaching the original and ultimate state of *Jade Pure* awareness. In my case, I spent over sixty years before I learned how to **abide** in heavenly Tao consciousness for at least three hours a day.

Books about mystical wisdom, like the Tao Te Ching, when authored by anyone other than a teacher who has reached *Jade Pure* Tao consciousness, will unfortunately always contain a sizeable number of incorrect assumptions, statements, theories, and translations.

As adeptly discussed by Harold. D. Roth in his excellent book *Original Tao*, he said that "mysticism has been uncritically used to refer to a wide variety of unusual human experiences from demonic visions to psycho-kinesis" by non-scholars.

Mr. Roth also describes the literary approach taken by trained scholars that are writing about ancient mysticism. In particular, he discusses the recent definitions articulated by philosopher Peter Moore.

Moore separates books about mystical writings into three distinct categories: "First-order books are individual, personal, accounts of mystical experiences; second-order books are scholarly interpretations in which the mystical experiences are described in abstract terms; and third-order books are interpretations of a mainly theological or literature-based analysis. These third-order books, although referring to some mystical object or reality do not refer, unless very obliquely, to the actual mystical experience itself."

Fortunately, this book in your hands is based on first-order personal mystic experiences of the highest levels of *Jade Pure* Tao awareness. It's time to sit back, relax and fasten your seatbelts.

The Jade Sages of Ancient Taoism

The mystical Taoist path that slowly emerged before the Chinese dynasties was not a shamanistic practice, a philosophy, or a religion. It was a truly mystic path that taught Taoist followers the yellow dragon Way to Heaven. It taught people how to meditate on Tao consciousness, beyond mind-body awareness, in order to reach the highest levels of *Jade Pure* mystical awareness.

The ancient Taoists sages most likely used their jade tablets to meditate on, and to teach Taoism to new followers. There are dozens of different types of jade tablets that we will cover in Chapter 8.

I've been teaching mystic meditation on clear awareness for over fifty years, and I can easily teach the entire path to divine Celestial Awareness by just using these Taoist tablets.

In fact, several ancient Taoist wisdom teachings were totally lost and forgotten, and never taught again, over the past five thousand years. But I have begun to teaching these same ancient lessons again.

This is not only the oldest known direct-consciousness path that was ever taught on Earth, but it is one of the most important, and advanced, mystic paths.

In the heavenly realms, a fully enlightened Taoist mystic, while still in a state of celestial, *Jade Pure* consciousness can experience: the resting consciousness that exists before, during and after the Cosmos (i.e., the ten thousand things); the initial creation process of the cosmos, the creation of new dimensions, solar systems, planets, animals, and sentient beings; the creation of energy, life, and sound waves from consciousness;

the one-in-many-and-many-in-one nurturing, replenishing, and sharing of Tao consciousness with countless trillions of other "bubbles" of clear awareness;and much, much more.

These are the types of experiences that many of the most ancient Taoist saints obviously had before and during the Hsi, Shang, and Zhou dynasties. These great, immortal sages could not have described and taught the seminal mystic Taoist teachings, unless they had previously reached these same celestial levels of *Jade Pure* awareness.

I know all of this from personal meditation experiences that enabled me to effortlessly and immediately understand ancient, mystical Taoism. In Chapter 8, I will explain these kinds of experiences in greater depth, as we further explore the ancient, mystic Taoist teachings.

These are, unmistakably, rare experiences. Of the many tens of thousands of gurus and spiritual teachers who exist today, I seriously doubt that there are more than a handful of celestially enlightened saints/teachers who have had, and continue to have, the full range of these kinds of experiences.

But every human on Earth has the natural ability to become a mystic and to eventually travel through the entire path of Celestial Awareness. Mystics are, simply, ordinary people who have taken the time to deeply explore divine awareness.

It takes a poet to understand another poet. It takes a scientist to understand another scientist. It takes a scholar to understand another scholar. Likewise, it takes a celestial mystic to understand another celestial mystic.

Given this truth, it is easy to see that only another true mystic has the spiritual ability to understand, and accurately describe, the enlightened teachings of any other previous mystic path — like ancient mystic Taoism.

I am grateful to have been able to travel the entire mystic path in this lifetime, and equally grateful for the opportunity to explain the mystic path of Tao consciousness.

I've studied and treasured hundreds of beautiful, interesting, inspirational books on Taoism by professional poets, scholars, psychologists, philosophers, teachers, scientists, sinologists, archaeologists, and historians. And I owe a great debt to the various authors of these books.

The wealth of knowledge in these wonderful books is truly amazing. But most of these books fail to accurately explore and describe the complete mystical underpinnings and wisdom of ancient Taoism, and that's why I'm writing this book.

I'm just a simple mystic — an old man with an ancient mystic teaching to share that might be of interest to you.

Through seminars, spiritual retreats, and podcasts, I've taught various meditation methods and ancient wisdom to more than ten thousand spiritually minded people over the past fifty years, but I intuitively waited until now to start teaching mystic Taoism.

It's time now for me to hit the reset button on the recent avalanche of spiritual misinformation. It's time for candid discussions about real mysticism. Thus, this is also the best time to review and discuss the ancient, original path of Tao consciousness.

The Vital Essence

Original Tao consciousness (in other words, Celestial Awareness) is the vital essence of cosmic Tao. It is the essence of motion and, thus, energy. It is the essence of subatomic particles, which are just tiny streams of energy. It is thus the essence of molecules that are nothing more than small fields of sub-atomic particles. It is thus the essence of matter which is nothing more than large fields of molecules.

It is the essence of the gravity wells that form in the center of every energy spiral. It is the essence of the stillness that manifests in these gravity wells. It is the essence of the consciousness that manifests in this stillness. It is the essence of life that flows from and as new consciousness. It is our essence, or original nature, that exists at the very core of our consciousness.

Original Tao consciousness is thus the essence of all things.

I first saw spiraling energy patterns as a teenager – watching energy form out of pure awareness and then spiraling outward, eventually creating molecules and tiny little gravity centers.

The spiraling energy pattern is commonly found in hundreds of different flowers, shells, rocks, and other aspects of nature. But it is much more amazing and meaningful to be able to watch as energy appears out of nowhere just before it begins to spiral.

The great impressionist painter Vincent Van Gogh also seemed to have seen the spiraling energy patterns in the air – illustrated in his *Starry Night* painting.

In the same way that spiraling energy can seemingly appear out of nowhere, new regions of Tao consciousness can easily appear within the clear awareness of a Taoist mystic.

How Does a Mystic Describe Tao?

True mystics describe Tao from their inner experiences of Tao. That's true today, it was true three hundred years ago, and it is apparent to me that it was true three thousand years ago in ancient China as well.

In the early days of the Hsia dynasty, the word *Tao* had a wide range of multiple meanings. It was used to describe the way to Heaven, the Taoist meditation practice, Tao consciousness, the original heavenly nature, the luminant, ether-like consciousness that flows from the heavens through every individual and the heavenly creator of all things.

The following views on mystic meditation come from both personal experience as well as from discussions from many other mystics that cross-validated my meditation experiences.

Mystics meditate on the pure, clear awareness that exists far beyond all mind-body and time-space awareness — which can also be called celestial consciousness, Tao, or Qi.

In highly enlightened states of meditation, a mystic can reach the nexus point. This is a hidden region of consciousness on the borderline between the mind-body microcosm of mind-body awareness and the heavenly, cosmic macrocosm. This is also the point where the celestial conscious, or Tao, flows into the clear awareness of humans.

Within the nexus point, true Taoist mystics discover that their very awareness, their lifeforce, and their energy is constantly flowing into them from some higher source within the cosmos. It's like you're born again, every microsecond.

At deeper levels beyond the hidden region called the Nexus Point, you begin to sense the creative capabilities of Tao, as it constantly re-creates your body and your mind.

The Heavenly Regions of Tao Consciousness

Much later, in even deeper levels of Tao consciousness, a true mystic is able to reach the *Jade Pure* region of heavenly consciousness. The ancient Taoists simply refer to this great region as Tao or as Zaohua (the creative aspect of Tao).

Most Christian religions also refer to this great region as heaven, but further define and deify the ultimate heavenly consciousness as God or as Our Father in Heaven. And most Christian religions consider heaven to be something like a huge planet that is heavily populated with Christians, angels, and one single God.

However, there are no planets in the regions beyond mind-body awareness. There is just celestial consciousness, or Tao, that may be defined either as one great region of pure consciousness or as several different regions of consciousness.

Like the ancient Taoists, most modern Vedic, Hindu, Sikh, and Radha Soami saints also contend that heaven is a region of pure consciousness. They then subdivide the region of heaven into multiple different regions of celestial consciousness. Saint Kabir and Saint Guru Nanak often talked about the existence of eighteen different regions of consciousness, but they did not carefully or thoroughly define these actual regions.

Like Kabir and others, I have also identified multiple different regions of clear awareness — regions that exist beyond all mind-body awareness. Based on over sixty years of intensive meditation on Tao consciousness and driven by the needs of most contemporary seekers who require substantially greater detail, I have carefully defined every different region of integral, transpersonal (e.g, beyond mind-body awareness) consciousness. I'm also currently working on a new book entitled *The 22 Levels of Transpersonal Consciousness*, which will contain complete descriptions and requirements of these regions.

This book should be available sometime in 2023.

The Creative "Big Bang" Power of Tao

As discussed above, the Taoist creative vortex, or the aspect of Tao that creates the ten thousand things, is *Zaohua* in Chinese. In the human body, it is simply called *Qi*.

This creative power is named God the Creator in Christian religions, or Brahma in many Hindu and Vedic paths. In recent years, Nisargadatta has referred to this same creative aspect of clear consciousness as the supreme guru within you.

In the same vein, Captain Ji has called it the Super Being of pure consciousness, and Ramana has referred to it as the supreme consciousness or as *sat-chit-ananda-bliss*. Soami Ji, the original founder of the Radha Soami path, more appropriately called it the lord of the soul. *Radha Soami* in the Sanskrit language means "lord of the soul."

Each one of these gurus talked about the core of our soul as a *fractal* copy of the Zaohua creative vortex in heaven.

There are uncountable billions of planets in the physical world, but every fully enlightened mystic will tell you that there is only one primary, or central creative vortex, located at the cosmic source of all consciousness, that creates new universes and planets.

The current consensus among astronomers is that there are an estimated one hundred billion galaxies in the universe, each containing about a billion trillion stars. Therefore, according to Erik Zackrisson, an astrophysicist in Sweden, "given our understanding of the universe and the laws of physics, there should be 70 quintillion planets in the current universe."

Most astrophysicists believe that most of these current planets came from a single "big bang," but they still don't know what that big bang was, or if it still exists.

Like most biophysicists, they agree that nature is a complex cosmic-wide web of fractal patterns and creative forces. However, they just don't know exactly what started, and what continues, this cosmic-wide web of creation. In recent years, a small percentage of modern scientists have theorized that some sort of conscious power is conceivably responsible for every instance of consciousness as well as every created thing.

However, zaohua, or supreme consciousness, is neither a human-like creator nor a god. It is a cosmic-wide celestial consciousness that is constantly, effortlessly, creating many different types of things from, as, and through the original nature of pure "Tao" awareness.

And one of the celestial things that it creates is a fractal copy of itself as the core of our conscious soul.

The ancient Chinese mystical Taoists, much like Kabir, Guru Nanak, Soami Ji, and me have all "experienced" the creation of new souls — as fractal copies of the creative vortex while they themselves were meditating in the celestial creative vortex. This is why we, and other modern saints like Ramana and Nisargadatta, have all passionately declared that heavenly consciousness is also at the very core of human awareness.

It's not just an abstract philosophical theory or a literary concept. For us, it's an experience.

Within this divine awareness, true mystics are vividly awake as the creators of the ten thousand things, and as the inner created consciousness, the energy, the molecules, the molecular structures, and the abundant space within all objects and sentient beings. This is not something that the human mind can comprehend.

A true mystic is also fully aware of Celestial Awareness, the entire creation process, the limited awareness of the new soul, the visions/experiences that the new soul encounters, and even the Tao consciousness of the cosmic space surrounding the new soul.

In simple terms, a fully enlightened monk can experience the creation of his/her own existence from and as clear, creative, heavenly source awareness.

It's also important to understand that consciousness is an integral dimension of many different levels of experience. Thus, the highest regions of consciousness subsume all of the lower fields of consciousness.

From decades of mystic experience, it is abundantly clear to me that the highly advanced mystic powers one gains from learning how to abide in the highest causal planes and heavenly regions are permanent.

Being able to stay still and wide awake at the core of any level of consciousness enables mystics to (1) go to any field of consciousness in the blink of an eye; (2) watch the entire light show (of exploding stars, streaks, rivers of light, enlightened consciousness, and huge seas of light) while they're meditating; and (3) experience life in multiple levels/dimensions of consciousness at the same time.

The ancient Taoist mystics didn't need scientific theories. They knew from experience (1) how the ten thousand cosmic things were created and (2) how the creative process within their souls created and continues to create the virtual matrix that they experience daily.

These celestially enlightened mystics are very rare. They are obviously able to clearly understand and carefully explain the ancient mystical Taoist teachings and meditation practices.

Tao Is Neither Water nor Breath

Lao Tzu sometimes used the notion of water to symbolize Tao as it flowed through humans — from the crown chakra, through the eye center and then downward through the rest of the body. But it is Tao consciousness that is flowing through the body, not water. Lao Tzu was simply speaking poetically.

In the early meditative stages, clear Tao awareness often appears to be like a shimmering, luminant nectar, or lake, as you enter clear consciousness. The great Persian poet-saints Hafiz and Rumi often referred to it as a golden nectar or as a divine wine. Likewise, Guru Nanak often referred to it as the pure white sea of existence. But it's just a mental phenomenon that you often see just before and/or after clear Tao consciousness.

Moreover, the Indian saints Tulsi Das, Babu Ji, Soami Ji, and Salig Ram, and I, have described the vast field of shimmering, high-energy, celestial Tao consciousness that feeds into the heavenly creative vortex as the Lake of Mansovar. It is, however, not a lake. All true mystics have abided in this field of Tao consciousness during deep meditations in the creative vortex. This field of consciousness is an energetic power that feeds into and enables the Creative Vortex.

I too am also guilty of using water as a symbolic metaphor. For about ten years, in my poetry and my podcasts, I have often described the Tao consciousness normally encountered in mystic meditation as streams of Celestial Awareness or as rivers of divine loving consciousness.

Mystics don't see, or hear, anything in clear Tao awareness. But in those few seconds while you're leaving the mind, or returning to the mind, you often see beautiful streaks of lights, vast pools of shimmering light, or bright, exploding stars of light. And just before you enter or leave clear awareness, you might hear some sounds emanating from your body.

Even in the first regions of mystic experiences, it becomes eminently evident that if you try to look at something, or listen to something, or memorize something, you will immediately lose your clear awareness as you drift back into the mind.

Starting in the first mystic region of consciousness in the eye center, many new mystic seekers will initially see something that slightly resembles a shimmering lake with a moon-like luster — just before they have the actual experience. However, once they effortlessly melt into clear awareness, the shimmering lake disappears.

The visions mystics have just before they enter or leave clear awareness at the eye center are much different in higher regions of Tao consciousness. Even so, the things we see through the mind, just before and after experiences of clear awareness, are similar, or identical, to the experiences of other mystics who have reached these same celestial regions.

As a Buddhist bodhisattva (Yeshe Nyingpo) in this life, I had the opportunity to compare notes with many great Buddhist teachers — including some of the same teachers that taught the Dalai Lama.

In the hidden region of the Cave of Brahma, for example, mystics will see thousands of bolts of lightning coming toward them, from all 360 degrees of perception. If the meditator watches or reacts to the crackling brilliance of any bolt of lightning, they will not be able to enter or stay in this region of clear awareness.

Similarly, just before a mystic enters any region of Tao consciousness, they might hear high-frequency sounds that have recently been described by several Indian gurus as celestial sounds.

They might hear high-pitched sounds, the sounds of a bell, the sounds of a sitar, or the sounds of thunder. They may be described as celestial sounds, but these sounds are simply coming from the human body, or from sound waves traveling through the space near the meditator's body.

Some spiritually minded religions mistakenly claim that these celestial sounds are coming from higher heavenly regions, and that if you hear them, it's evidence that you've reached a heavenly region.

But the truth is that you can actually hear these so-called celestial sounds even before you enter the mystic third-eye experience. But if you make a conscious mental effort to try to grasp, remember, or listen to any of these sounds, you will be prevented from entering or staying in clear awareness.

Following Breath toward Clear Awareness

Many modern hatha yoga and Taoist paths currently believe that Qi (or Chi), is the fabled Taoist vital essence and therefore new mystic seekers should practice different breathing exercise techniques. But anytime a person resorts to mental or physical practices for any length of time, they will not be able to have mystic experiences during that "mental" time frame.

However, there is a small shred of truth concerning the use of breath — just *before* you enter states of pure awareness. You can use breath effortlessly to relax so deeply that you sometimes melt into regions of clear awareness. However, it must happen effortlessly, or naturally, without mental awareness.

It doesn't matter if you start your meditation session while you're in the mind. You just need to learn how to easily relax.

All mystic meditation experiences begin as you find a way to turn your conscious attention inward effortlessly, silently, and naturally. The great Saints Kabir, Guru Nanak and Soami Ji often referred to their mystic paths as Sahaj Yoga or Sahaja Yoga. *Sahaj* means "natural" or "effortless."

As mentioned above, a creative vortex lies at the core of every human's clear awareness. It's a fractal copy of the heavenly creative vortex that is often referred to as Tao or God the Creator or as the Lord of the Soul. The creative processes of both the divine heavenly creative vortex and the core of the human soul are each acting instinctively in a natural, effortless manner. The soul always naturally travels within the streams of Tao energy patterns.

The soul instinctively follows the Tao energy when it is moving outward into the mind that creates/paints the outside virtual-matrix dream world of our everyday life.

The soul, likewise, naturally, and instinctively follows the Tao energy inward-return-path back to the core of its soul.

Mentally following, or examining, your consciousness always interferes with the instinctive, natural movements of the soul.

You can automatically achieve eye-center enlightenment when you "naturally" discontinue the mental process. Once you gently and tenderly stop thinking, desiring, doing, trying, looking, hearing, feeling, remembering, imagining, or measuring, you will be able to experience enlightenment when your soul is ready for that experience.

So, how does your breathing become helpful when you're on your way from the mind (fragmented awareness) to the soul (clear, Tao awareness)?

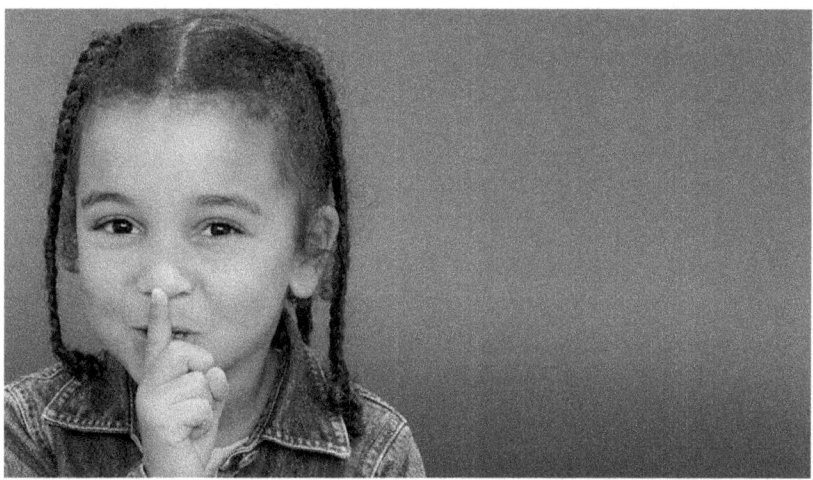

The answer is that it is sometimes helpful to simply allow the attentive aspect of your *quiet and still awareness* to naturally follow your inward breath as it moves up and into your head. Stay within your awareness, and effortlessly follow as a silent observer — without grasping for it or analyzing it.

Third-Eye Enlightenment

As you get close to the eye center, while naturally following your breath, you will begin to feel an increase in the density of your consciousness and the vibrations of a new field of energy.

All this happens in the gap of silence between the inbreath and the outbreath. As this happens, your attention is no longer on your breathing at all. Instead, there is an automatic tendency for your soul awareness to begin to look inward toward the very source of your Tao awareness.

Whenever your attention gets near the eye-center chakra, it awakens the chakra. When your third-eye chakra begins to awaken, it always vibrates and expands outward in streams of spiraling energy. The combination of the spiraling energy and the increased vibrations makes your consciousness feel denser than before.

It's critical, at this point, to ignore your mind-body feelings. This is an important mystic secret.

The trick is to tenderly let your attentive awareness naturally drift into the center of your awareness. When your soul is ready to be mystically enlightened, it will instinctively, and automatically, place its attention at the very center of your awareness. You don't have to do anything at all by yourself.

With practice, this entire sequence of following your awareness inward and back to its source will happen automatically – in less than the blink of an eye.

A Zen koan is a puzzle or paradoxical statement Buddhists use as a teaching tool while meditating to uncover truths using the intuitive mind rather than the intellect. One of my favorite Zen kaons is: "In clear awareness, thoughts and emotions will sometimes come and go. Let them. Just don't stop to serve them tea."

The overarching secret of mystic meditation is to do nothing. Just effortlessly, blissfully, and gratefully ignore everything except clear awareness. Eventually, occasional thoughts and emotions won't distract you at all.

A highly advanced mystic can stay in Tao awareness without noticing his or her breath for hours, days, or weeks at a time.

Such a mystic can do this while sitting on a cushion (e.g., a sitting meditation) or while effortlessly walking about in the world (e.g., wu wei). When this sharp, clear, blissful awareness lasts for weeks, or months, it is called *samadhi*.

In higher regions of consciousness, your soul's clear Tao awareness will enter an intimate relationship with the celestial Tao awareness that is in everything, and as everything that you experience in the virtual matrix of mind-body awareness.

Within the very air, and in the subtle energy patterns in the air, you will experience the same Tao consciousness. Likewise, within every object, and every molecule of every object, you will also experience the same

Tao consciousness —without ever losing your attentive, effortless awareness of Tao.

As the Crown Chakra Opens

As your third-eye chakra vibrates, it sends electromagnetic signals to your interconnected heart chakra and your crown chakra, causing them to awaken and spiral.

Weeks, months, or sometimes years after learning how to abide for long stretches of time at the eye center, you will often effortlessly notice the stream of enlightened consciousness that is already flowing from the top of your head and then dissolving into your eye-center consciousness.

It's a common mistake, among new seekers, to believe that this is a new stream of consciousness. But it's actually not new at all. It is, more accurately, the same stream of vital energy consciousness that has always been flowing into your body and then into your eye-center awareness while you have been alive.

The ancient Vedic term for this stream of vital energy is *prana*. It flows silently through your entire body in the same way your blood does. It primarily travels through a network of energy lines, but it also travels through your veins. It is not breath or blood even though it might feel as though it is.

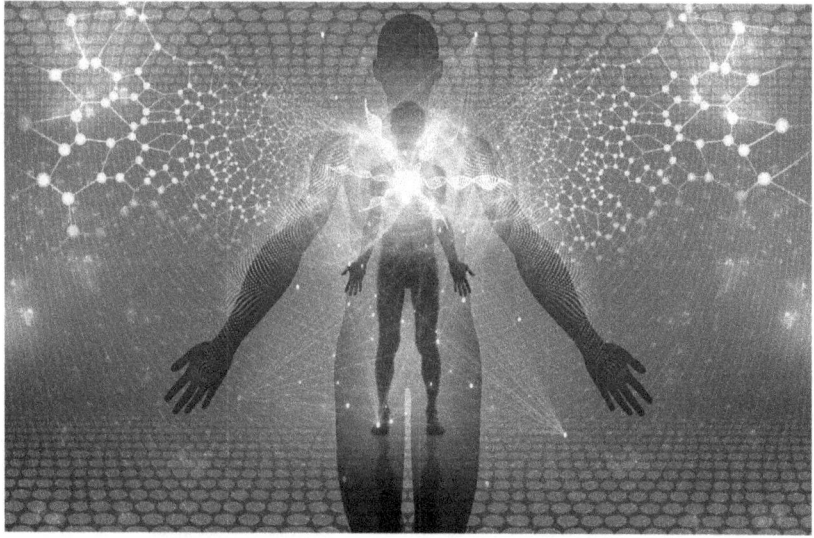

From a mind-body awareness, it initially seems as if these waves of purer crown-chakra consciousness are entering and mixing with your breath, but that's not actually what is happening. Anytime you take a normal, deep breath, you can cognitively feel the energetic vibrations in your body as you breathe outward.

Likewise, when your consciousness is traveling through the same energetic pathways from your head and then through your body, it creates a similar mental feeling in your body that resembles your breath when it takes the same route from your head to your chest.

And this is exactly why most non-mystic thinkers get confused about the nature of Tao when it was described as vital energy, or vital essence, about three thousand years after the beginning of the ancient mystical Taoist path.

Your body is a physical covering around your consciousness. Your true Tao consciousness exists before, during, and after the body. Your body is created by your consciousness, which continues to flow through your body, while your body is alive.

The nature of Tao is not confusing in mystic awareness. It is confusing in mind-body awareness.

At much higher levels of mystic consciousness, you can witness the ongoing creation of your own body – from this pure white, energetic Tao awareness that many ancient Chinese philosophers came to call Qi.

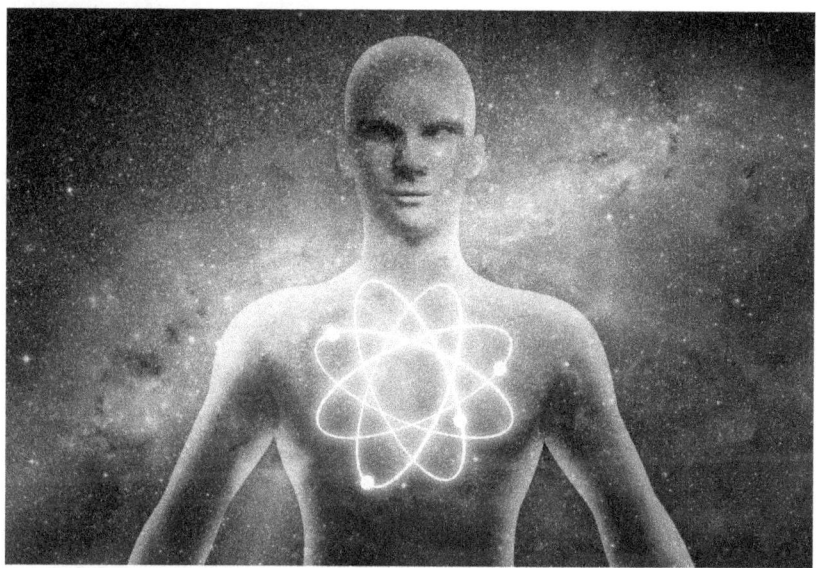

Tao, Qi, Tian, and Zhohua

The word *qi* (or *chi*) is currently being used by some Taoist organizations to describe the conscious current of Tao when it flows through the human form, empowering life, energy, and wisdom.

To an evolved mystic, however, there are no major differences between the words Tao, qi, chi, or zhohua. These are all states of Tao consciousness – with some differences in the quality, or intensity, of experience. Nor is there any difference between Tao consciousness and descriptive terms like heaven *tian* (heaven) *tian-wen* (heavenly patterns), *tien-hsing* (heavenly nature).

As previously mentioned, within the creative vortex, Tao re-creates itself into new streams of Tao consciousness, which then eventually become the other ten thousand things, or all things. The Chinese-language term for this process is *zaohua*. However, during every stage of the zaohua process, the core Tao consciousness remains the same.

Most people get confused about the nature of Tao. What is it? What is it at different levels of consciousness?

But for highly advanced mystics there is no confusion at all. Tao is always Tao consciousness, even when it might appear to the mind as any one of the ten thousand different solid objects. A true mystic can often experience the Tao consciousness within the trillions of molecules that exist within everyday objects.

Unfortunately, many philosophers and historians have also been confused and mistaken about the real meaning of qi. They quite often either talk about it in abstract terms or define it as some sort of heavenly breath. Neither of these theories describe the true, original nature of Tao, or qi. Your breath remains breath, which like everything else, including your own awareness, is always Tao consciousness. Your breath, just like your thoughts, doesn't mix with Tao. They *are* Tao.

It is impossible to understand what Tao is, and what it is at different levels of Tao consciousness, without traveling the mystic path of Tao consciousness and learning how to abide — for very long periods of time — in all twenty-two levels of human and divine Tao consciousness.

A mystical meditative life is a discovery process that begins with wu wei when you originally learn to float as a silent observer and eventually enables you to learn how to effortlessly melt into your original nature as pure Tao consciousness.

Mystical Tao consciousness begins at the eye center, rests halfway at the crown chakra, and eventually completes its sojourn in the resting, or source, state of heavenly cosmic consciousness.

Once you learn how to abide in the eye center for three to ten hours at a time, without ever moving about or thinking, you're typically ready to melt into higher regions of Tao consciousness.

By the time you reach the crown chakra, you can easily abide in samadhi (an intense state of still awareness) for several days, or even weeks, at a time.

By the time that you reach the resting, or source state of Tao consciousness, you will have learned how to abide for many months, years, or even decades at a time.

Fully enlightened Taoist mystics can achieve all of this in a single lifetime. Moreover, even when they're in their minds, a true mystic can effortlessly melt into creative consciousness or into source consciousness in less time than it takes to blink.

As noted by many other saints that I've talked to, more than 99 percent of the "spiritual teachers" on Earth don't seem to have even reached the eye center (the first stage of mystic awareness). They, as well, cannot understand Tao.

These wannabes can read hundreds of books and listen to hundreds of podcasts from different mystics, but without real, abiding experiences in the deepest levels of *Jade Pure* heavenly Tao consciousness, they will not be able to understand what Tao consciousness actually is.

Without fully enlightened mystic experiences, most ancient and modern spiritual teachers, sinologists, philosophers, historians, poets, and scholars have not and will not be able to comprehend the real meaning of terms like *Tao, qi, tian* and *zaohua*.

CHAPTER 7

WHAT IS TAO CONSCIOUSNESS?

As discussed in Chapter 6, the very first state, or bubble, of Tao consciousness is much different from normal mind-body awareness, which consists of trains of thought that are highly fragmented around personal perspectives and personal memories.

In contrast, Tao consciousness is a transpersonal awareness that is beyond personal mind-body, and space-time, perspectives and experiences. It is also beyond what most spiritual and consciousness teachers describe as spiritual enlightenment.

What Is Spiritual Enlightenment?

The term *spiritual enlightenment* is confusing to most of us on the spiritual path because it means different things to different people. The terms and definitions vary over the map. Who's right? Is anyone right?

Moreover, does it really matter if your personal definition is different from someone else's? The only thing that matters is whether it works for you.

The good news here is that everyone is always right from their own perspective. If a person's spiritual path makes them happier and more spiritually oriented, then it's a fantastic path for them.

Spiritual enlightenment is a journey of many progressively beautiful discoveries, and people's experiences as well as their definitions are always changing.

After over fifty years of reading spiritual doctrines, meditating for at least 3 hours a day, and teaching thousands of new seekers, I've learned a lot about spiritual enlightenment and spiritual paths. One of the most valuable observations I've made is that definitions change over time as both new and old seekers make progress on the path.

As you gain more experience, your definitions change. It doesn't really matter who's right and who's wrong. If your spiritual lifestyle works for you, then it's always an exceptionally beautiful path. It's about letting go of the old you and enjoying the new, more spiritual you.

For most new seekers, any spiritual practice that helps them to become progressively more loving, blissful, harmonious, or peaceful, while also helping them to become less egotistical, less emotional, and less attached to worldly things is a great personal practice to follow. As life becomes more beautiful, most newbies also passionately believe they have been spiritually enlightened.

It's a different bag for experienced seekers. These practitioners have gone both deeper and longer into stretches of blissful, non-cognitive, clear awareness. When they're sitting around the lunch table together, you will often hear them referring to this new seeker's initial stage simply as a stepping stone, albeit a spiritually driven, vital one to true spiritual enlightenment.

And then there are the divine stages of enlightenment, which are indescribably beautiful.

At this far end of the spectrum, highly advanced mystic seekers have a much more seasoned perspective.

During the last eight thousand years, the most advanced mystics have all had a remarkably similar definition for enlightened awareness. They all basically describe it as a clear, blissful awareness that is never cluttered with thoughts, emotions, mind-body awareness, or personal perspectives. It was their soulful experiences, beyond mind-body awareness, that led them to see things this way.

Most seekers never reach true eye-center enlightenment. In fact, most gurus and so-called spiritual teachers never reach eye-center enlightenment, no matter how much they charge for their "spiritual awakening" courses.

In a real eye-center enlightenment, all types of thoughts, emotions, and mind-body awareness just don't happen. What happens instead are significantly increased levels of clarity of awareness, bliss, oneness, love, equipoise, harmony, peace, freedom, and a sense of the divine presence. In the beginning it seems like a tenfold increase in all these characteristics. At even deeper levels of "heavenly" clear awareness, the magnitude factor can feel millions of times higher.

Choosing Some Easy Definitions

To make things easy for readers, I'm going to use the following common definitions about the four different stages of spiritual enlightenment.

Any person who reaches any one of these four distinct stages becomes more enlightened than they were before. And that's a very good thing! Every one of these stages is a precious stepping-stone on the path to enlightened human awareness. The subsequent increase in enlightened awareness not only helps us as individuals, but it also helps to awaken the world in which we live.

1. Spiritually Driven

The first stage of this beautiful path to Celestial Awareness can be referred to as spiritually driven. In the beginning of this journey, it's a path full of many wonderful new mysteries that seem to beg for a greater analysis and an even greater number of questions.

When we reach this early stage of heightened awareness, we may begin to share our experiences with our best friends (BFFs) and our close-knit tribe. It's the stage when we go online to look up dozens of unfamiliar terms and to explore dozens of new mystical practices. It often drives us to find other like-minded souls.

As we begin to answer some of our new questions, we also start to become less judgmental, more accepting, less reactionary, less emotional, and more compassionate to others. As this happens, our enhanced attitudes and habits not only help us, but they also positively affect our friends and family.

2. Spiritually Minded

In the next phase of the path, we begin to become more spiritually minded. At this stage in our journey, we've begun to develop a spiritual lifestyle that helps us become more focused on inward experiences instead of the worldly experiences. By this point, we are typically spending an hour or more every day practicing our favorite meditation techniques. We will also have begun to explore many different types of meditation practices and teachers. We become more easygoing and less attached to our old desires and fears.

One of the hallmarks of this beautiful phase is that we begin to relish, and even love, periods of stillness and silence. While we're in these periods of silence, we often notice a slightly blissful feeling and a greater connection to everything around us. By tenderly observing while floating, over time we begin to notice that we feel more loved and emptier.

Once we learn how to effortlessly abide in this mental silence, we can sometimes reach the gap between our trains of thought. Although everything seems still, it's because we are still tightly holding on to this gap of awareness. Eventually we learn that it's a gap of silence that exists before and after every train of thought. At this stage, however, we just don't know what to do about it yet.

There are countless sincere contemporary teachers who unfortunately describe this gap as true enlightenment, the *be here now* enlightenment, universal awareness, or as coherent alignment with God consciousness. But when we're still holding on to any experience in awareness, then we're still in the mind, where we can become even more attached to our thoughts and our memories.

Becoming spiritually minded is a precious milestone in personal development. Nonetheless, most true mystics clearly understand that true enlightenment happens in the next stage — where there's absolutely no mind-body awareness occurring at all.

3. Spiritually Enlightened

A spiritually enlightened person is someone who has experienced a bubble, or field, of clear, non-personal, non-cognitive, blissful awareness, and has then been able to abide (to effortlessly rest) in that awareness for several minutes or several hours at a time.

The first stage of true spiritual enlightenment typically happens at the eye center. During this experience, there is absolutely no mind-body awareness, no personal perspective, no thoughts, and no emotions of any kind. Grasping, or trying to hold on to the slightest thought or perception will immediately destroy your ability to stay in this bubble of clear spiritually enlightened awareness.

It's also a stage of incredible differences between your old mental awareness and your new spiritually enlightened awareness. As mentioned above, in this stage your clarity of awareness; your concentration in awareness; your senses of peace, freedom, love, and divine presence are all about ten times greater than ever before.

4. Divinely Enlightened

The last stage of divinely enlightened experiences occurs once we go entirely beyond every single aspect of personal, and even soulful awareness. When that happens, we subsequently merge into *the ONE* celestial, or heavenly, awareness that is always nurturing, loving, supporting, and re-creating every other aspect of consciousness in the universe.

The very subtle notion that I-AM a soul instantly dissolves as our consciousness is replaced by the divine consciousness that was and still is the true nature of all humans.

This is also an indescribable, multi-dimensional experience that contains and subsumes every other lower level of transpersonal awareness.

Because the highest level of divine enlightenment subsumes every other level of spiritual awareness, it is also referred to as *integral consciousness*.

Everything that is experienced through divine awareness is a permanent experience and can be accessed at any time in the future.

About six thousand years ago, the ancient Taoists referred to this final stage as *Jade Pure* Tao consciousness. Buddha referred to this last stage of divine enlightenment as Nirvana. The Sanskrit Veda gurus referred to it as the resting consciousness. Later Vedic mystics also referred to it as Brahma. Christ, in the teaching of Saint John, referred to it as the Word of God. Kabir often referred to it as source consciousness. Soami Ji, in modern times, called this type of spiritual enlightenment the Lord of the Soul or as Radha Soami awareness. Ramana referred to it as Sat-Chit-Ananda-Bliss. I usually refer to this final stage as either divine awareness, Celestial Awareness, or as source consciousness.

Twenty-Two Levels of Spiritual Enlightenment

After carefully mapping every different level of consciousness, I have observed that there appear to be around twenty-two distinct levels of spiritual enlightenment – starting with the eye- center enlightenment and ending in source consciousness.

In each of these different regions of spiritual enlightenment, your consciousness becomes significantly more resonant and coherently aligned with the true nature of divine awareness.

Along the way within, your consciousness will exhibit new characteristics. Furthermore, the miracles you observe in your daily life will become more amazing and more frequent. Inevitably, you will eventually understand what it means to "be in this world but not of it."

Several great, ancient, and modern mystics including Kabir, Guru Nanak, Tulsi Das and Soami Ji, likewise believed that eighteen distinct levels of Spiritual Enlightenment exist. However, none of these saints ever defined these regions.

In future essays, podcasts, and books, I will continue to discuss each one of these twenty-two different celestial regions of spiritually enlightened and divinely enlightened consciousness. Along the way, I invite you to ask any questions that you have and to share your new wisdom with your best friends and your tribe.

You are not just in the universe; your consciousness is the universe. You are not just a person, but a focal point where the universe is becoming more conscious of itself.

Spiritual enlightenment is an amazing miracle — at every level of progress!

CHAPTER 8

TAO-CHIH-TAO POEMS

The following ancient Taoist Jade tablets were used in ancient China to teach the mystic path of Tao consciousness.

Sometimes the jade sages used a single tablet to discuss something. At other times, it appears that they used several tablets to form a sentence.

Having taught this path before in several different lifetimes, I'm going to teach it in this chapter now in a similar way that the Tao Te Ching, the Tai Shang Gan Ying Pian, and the Nei-Yeh were taught. I will use a combination of short poems that describe the basic principles occasionally followed by supplemental explanations.

Tao Cosmology

Most great religions were initially started by a divinely enlightened sage who knew how to explain the new mystic path from a celestially enlightened perspective.

This is true with Buddhism, Christianity, Sikhism, Sant Mat, Radha Saomi, and Taoism. The creation beliefs and the meditation practices were also very similar.

Lord Buddha, in his first sermon, taught that everything was created by Nirvana/heavenly (source) consciousness, and that the way back to heavenly awareness was through a life devoted to "that which never comes and goes" (Nirvana/Thagatta Consciousness).

Yeshua (Jesus Christ) taught that the Word (divine consciousness) created the entire cosmos including humans who were created as a fractal copy (image) of divine consciousness (Word/Holy Spirit), and could be realized by lifelong devotion to their inner spirit.

Kabir, the founder of Sant Mat, taught that the supreme consciousness (Ashabd, or soundless-sound) created the entire cosmos, including humans who were created as a fractal copy of divine consciousness (Ashabd). He taught that every man or woman, through passionate meditation on inner consciousness, could eventually achieve supreme consciousness as well.

Guru Nanak, the founder of the Sikh religion and a follower of Kabir's teaching, taught that the formless-form, and soundless-sound of divine consciousness, was the creator of everything and was thus both the supreme being of the cosmos and the Lord of the soul. He also taught that by deeply listening through the soul's consciousness in the inner Court of the Lord, humans could achieve divine enlightenment.

Soami Ji, the founder of the Radha Soami/Sant Mat path, taught that Radha Soami (the Lord of the Soul) was a divine consciousness and the Lord Creator of every soul, which also contained an inner guru copy of the Radha Soami consciousness.

Based on the ancient Taoist teachings of the jade sages, Lao Tzu, Tai Shang, T'ien P'ien, and Zuangzi, the original divine Tao consciousness (vital essence) created everything (the ten thousand things) and can be fully realized by inward meditation on Tao consciousness.

These early Taoist sages taught that Tao, as the original source-creator of everything and as the only thing that never comes and goes, is the inward vital essence within every human; and, by holding on the Tao, one will eventually merge into *Jade Pure* (heavenly) Tao consciousness.

Celestial Awareness

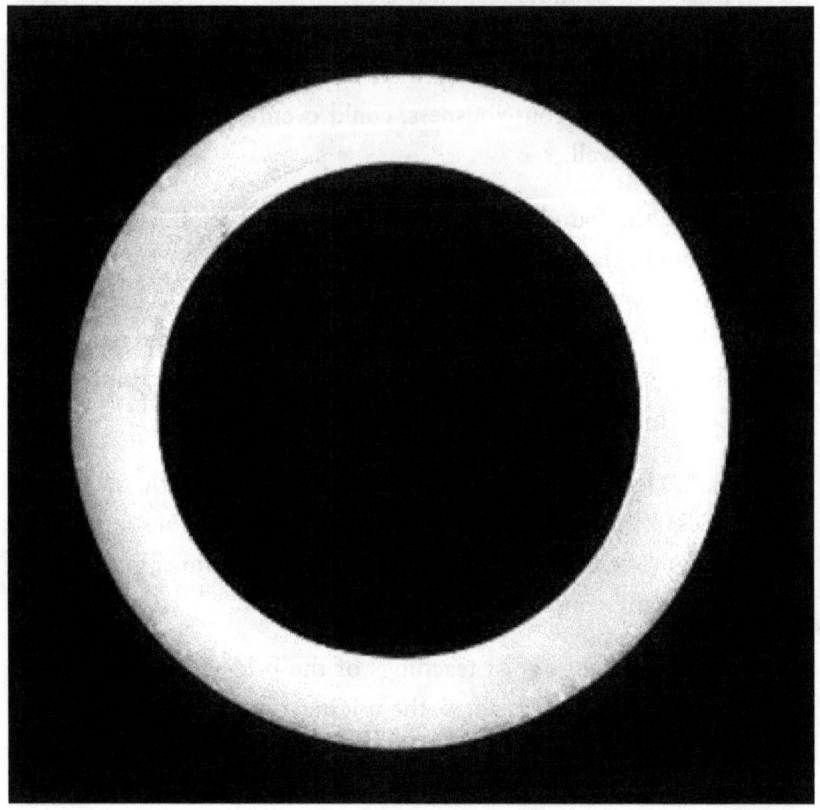

Tao is an everlasting instant of pure Celestial Awareness.

This is the everlasting instant of Tao consciousness.

It is an eternal, divine singularity of supreme awareness.

    It is the immortal creator of all space, energy, and things.

    It flows through, nurtures, and sustains all things.

    It compassionately regenerates everything.

    It creates everything in and as this everlasting instance.

    Celestial Awareness is the awareness of all beings.

Celestial Awareness is self-conscious in every inch of space, in every wave form, and in every object.

It is always one-in-all and all-in-one.

It is a singularity and a plurality of Celestial Awareness.

There is nothing that is not Tao.

It cannot be named.

But to explain it, we call it Tao.

The Everlasting Instant

Tao is the natural origin of all things.

This is Tao. This is Celestial Awareness.

All consciousness is Tao.

All sentient beings are internally Tao conscious.

Even mind-body awareness is Tao.

But mind-body awareness is ignorant of Tao.

Effortlessly looking inward towards Tao is Tao.

All energies and wave forms are Tao.

Light waves are Tao.

Sound waves are Tao.

The cosmic space that contains all things is Tao.

All "ten thousand" things are Tao.

There is nothing that is before, or beyond, Tao.

Heaven and Earth

In this everlasting instant:

Tao coexists as two Yin and Yang regions.

Yin, or Earth, is the region (s) of ten thousand things.

Yin is also the region of ten thousand worlds.

Yang, or heaven, is the region of celestial space.

Yang is the creative and connective power of Tao.

Singularity and Polarity

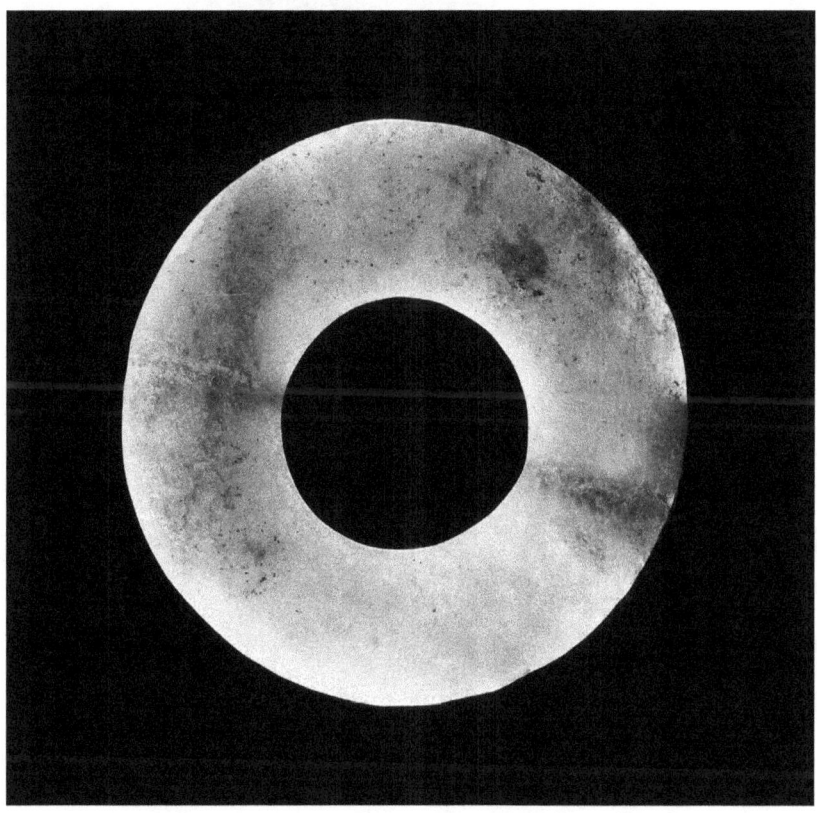

Tao is a conscious, cosmic singularity.

Tao is a conscious, cosmic plurality.

Tao is always the singularity and the plurality.

From within the Tao of singularity, plurality happens.

From within the Tao of plurality, singularity happens.

Below the crown chakra, Tao seems singular.

At the crown chakra, Tao seems like a plurality.

Heavenly Tao is always the singularity and the plurality.

Tao Saints abide in both singularity and plurality.

Tao Is Within Yin and Yang

Tao creates yin and yang and the Middle Way.

Tao is yin and yang and the Middle Way.

From within the Tao of yin, yang is created.

From within the Tao of yang, yin is created.

Creating duality on Earth, within heaven's Middle Way.

Dissolving as Tao in the heavens.

The Tao is the Tao, in Tao, and as Yin and Yang.

Tao Wind and Clouds

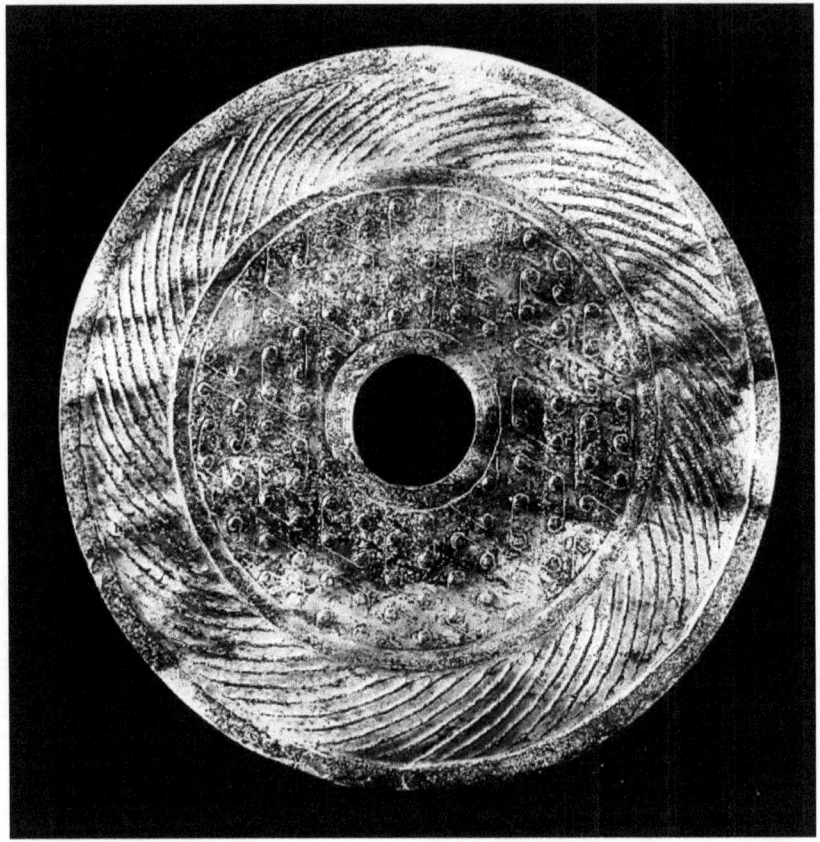

In the heavenly creative vortex Tao:

Moves outward creating the clouds and the wind.

That the yellow dragons need to use.

To help them to fly from Earth into the heavens.

Mystic Notes:

Tao flows eternally and timelessly throughout all the cosmic realms like a divine river, or a spring wind, of enlightened awareness. We name these small-to-huge flowing rivers of Tao consciousness **as the** *Winds of Tao Consciousness*.

As Tao consciousness flows through the cosmos, it occasionally creates small pools, ponds, lakes, and oceans of concentrated, harmonious, resonant Tao consciousness. We name these pools of awareness the *Clouds of Tao Consciousness.*

Abiding deeply within Tao awareness enables monks to become the totality of awareness in their Tao-cloud bubble of enlightenment.

Abiding in and as the Middle-Way enables monks to float in currents of Tao consciousness - like a leaf in a mountain stream or a butterfly in the wind.

Abiding in a river of Tao consciousness enables monks to melt into the wu wei river of Tao consciousness.

Tao comes and goes in an everlasting instant.

Tao, as everything, is always an everlasting instant.

There is no self or self-perception within Tao.

Thus, there is no space-time awareness within Tao.

Flowing through the middle way is wu wei.

Wu wei helps create Tao awareness in new students.

Abiding in Tao awareness enables new students to go beyond mind-body awareness.

Abiding in bubbles of enlightened Tao awareness enables monks to melt deep into bigger fields of Tao awareness.

Abiding as a totality of consciousness, in a state of harmonic equipoise, enables monks to go beyond awareness of awareness.

Heavenly Tao Creates Human Tao

 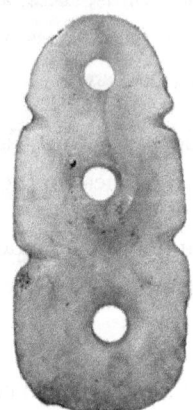

Just as the light of the sun can be seen on Earth.

Celestial Tao can be experienced within humans.

Tao flows continually into humans from the heavens.

Tao continually flows out of humans and then into the Earthly environment where humans live.

Tao is Celestial Awareness, mind-body awareness, clear awareness, soul consciousness, and the path back to *Jade Pure* Tao Consciousness.

Tao Becomes Four States

In this everlasting instant:

The Tao divides into the four states.

The yang of Qian(heaven) moves into the yin of Kun (Earth).

The yin of Kun (Earth) moves into Qian (heaven).

Qian entrusts its essence to Kun and becomes Li.

Kun receives that essence from Qian and becomes Kun.

The Tao is always: Yin, Yang, Li, Kun and Tao.

Flowing To and From Tao

In this everlasting instant:

Tao flows outward, and inward, in all directions.

As waves of Tao consciousness from and back to Tao.

It flows in all four directions.

It flows inward and outward (in 360 degrees).

It flows north, south, east and west (in 360 degrees).

It flows from and to Tao, in the middle as the origin of all.

Tao is everywhere at once, and nowhere to be found.

Tao Rises Like the Valley Mist

Tao rises up from the center of Celestial Awareness.

Like the valley mist flowing outward from its center.

Like the valley mist flowing outward from its source.

Spiraling outward into the cosmos to create all ten thousand things.

Spiraling as waves of Celestial Awareness named Chi.

Filled with magical Tao energy – like the ki seed.

Creating the ten thousand things of Tao Celestial Awareness.

Expanding the Celestial space to hold the ten thousand things.

A Cosmic Space of everlasting Tao Celestial Awareness.

The Illusionary World

In this everlasting instant of Tao consciousness.

The *Jade Pure* yellow dragon is the creative Tao.

Creating the ten thousand things from Tao consciousness.

Appearing like things to the unenlightened mind.

But experienced as Tao to the enlightened mind.

When we are one with Tao, we are Tao as we see Tao.

But in ignorance we only see an illusionary world.

In ignorance we think we are apart from Tao.

In ignorance we think that awareness arises from the mind.

In ignorance we depend on our mind instead of Tao.

In ignorance we live in a fragmented awareness.

In ignorance we live in emotional misery.

In ignorance we fear death and thus emptiness.

In Tao we live in highly enlightened bliss.

In Tao we live in an immortal, Celestial Awareness.

The Ocean and the Drop

Every soul is a drop of the cosmic ocean of Tao.

Every soul drops from the heavens to be born on Earth.

The soul and the ocean are interconnected.

The soul is always in the ocean.

And the ocean is always in the soul.

Tao Sages are always aware of the soul as ocean and as Tao.

Who Were the Yellow Dragons?

As mentioned in Chapter 2, the advent of shamans, with their religious visions, at the dawning of most great civilizations, has had a tremendous impact on many of the greatest religions on Earth — including the emergence of ancient Taoism.

The formative years of the great Chinese civilization from 8000 BCE to 2000 BCE evolved from hundreds of tiny villages, like Yubu, and from legendary shamans like Yu. The fabled shaman Yu was acclaimed as the architect who built the famous dragon gates that stopped the Yellow River from flooding. He was also lauded as the magical shaman who initially discovered the mystical yellow dragons.

The most influential tribal beliefs in ancient China included myths about the creation of the Earth by the gods in the sky, and more importantly the myths about the mystical yellow dragons who knew the secret ways to fly from Earth and into the center of the celestial heavens.

These same mystical myths about yellow dragons were used by the earliest Taoist sages. They suggested that a Taoist disciple could meditate on the heavenly Tao consciousness and eventually become like the fabled yellow dragon – who knew how to travel into the heavens.

During the years of the mystical Taoist path (5000–2000 BCE), the yellow dragon became a precious symbol for both a fully enlightened Taoist sage and for the creative consciousness within every Taoist disciple.

As mentioned above, the Taoist sages carved hundreds of jade tablets with images of the yellow dragon. Some tablets depicted the external Taoist stage as a yellow dragon. Other tablets used the illustration of an etched yellow dragon to describe the nature of the "inner guru" (yellow dragon) that would help every monk to find the necessary meditation secrets on the path to heavenly awareness.

During the path of Tao consciousness (2000–200 BCE), sages also carved hundreds of other tablets, without any yellow dragon symbolism. These were used to instruct advanced monks, and all Zhou-dynasty monks in how to meditate on Tao consciousness to achieve heavenly *Jade Pure* awareness.

The Huang Long Creates New Souls

Tao sages had full Tao consciousness in the womb.

Awake within the first molecule of the womb.

Like the yellow dragon they were heavenly awakened.

Awake they watched the creation process in the womb.

Watching the creation of new clouds (bubbles) of Tao.

Experiencing the winds/currents flowing through and around their bubbles of Tao consciousness.

Experiencing the heavenly wisdom at the core of their Tao.

Absorbed in Tao as Tao and the source of everything else.

Experiencing the density of Tao becoming lighter.

Becoming lighter still, to create two new molecules.

Becoming fully conscious in all three molecules.

As the same multi-dimensional Tao consciousness.

Dividing again and again into sixty-four molecules.

Fully Tao conscious in every molecule.

Watching the fetus grow into a baby.

Remembering what it was like to be source consciousness before the creation of the cosmos.

Remembering what it was like to divide into three realms of heavenly consciousness from source consciousness.

Remembering what it was like to be the source/resting Tao consciousness, the loving father of all consciousness and the mother/creator of all consciousness – all at the same time.

Remembering what it is like to create the ten thousand things.

Remembering what it is like to love the ten thousand things.

Remembering what it is like be in and as the ten thousand things.

Remembering what it is like to create a new soul.

Remembering what it was like to create this soul and to be this new yellow dragon.

Remembering how the new soul, which was created thousands of years ago, expanded in the same way that this yellow dragon fetus is expanding.

Remembering all of this in an everlasting instant of heavenly, *Jade Pure* Tao consciousness.

Activation of the Vital Essence

Yellow dragons are Tao consciousness.

Breathing in, they are filled with magical Tao consciousness.

Breathing out, they create new clouds of Tao.

Flying, they create winds of Tao.

And on the clouds and the winds they fly,

From Earth to heaven.... Through the celestial net.

Celestial Yellow Dragons

The magical yellow dragons are filled with Tao consciousness.

They fly from Earth and into the heavens through secret ways.

As they fly, they create new clouds of Tao consciousness.

As they fly, they create new streams of Tao consciousness.

Clouds and winds to mark the sacred Taoist ways to heaven.

Clouds and winds hiding this sacred path from everyone else with Tao awareness.

The Yellow Dragon Is Within You

The spirit of the yellow dragon is always within you.

The yellow dragon is waiting inside you to help you.

In Tao consciousness you can feel the yellow dragon.

In Tao consciousness you can fly with the yellow dragon.

When it gets to heaven it turns you into a yellow dragon.

This is how to become a heavenly, immortal yellow dragon.

Three Types of Souls

The ancient Taoist sages taught that there are three different kinds of souls born in the womb. There are worldly souls, marked souls, and jade sage souls.

For worldly souls, it is almost impossible to understand Tao consciousness and/or to follow the jade sage path.

Marked souls can feel the magic of the yellow dragons in their lives and are born with an urge to practice Tao consciousness.

Jade sage souls are born with full Tao consciousness and are destined to follow and teach the jade sage path.

Three Kinds of Souls in the Womb

Worldly Souls

Marked Souls

Jade Sage Souls

There are three different kinds of souls born in the womb.

Not every soul is the same when it enters the embryo.

Different souls are attracted to different paths and challenges.

New souls are heavily influenced by yin and yang forces/karmas.

New souls generally develop strong personalities.

New souls usually become attached to the world.

Older souls are less influenced by yin and yang energies.

They occasionally sense the divine presence of Tao.

They are more attracted to the Ch'ing spiritual energies.

The immortal sages are born in wu-chi Tao awareness.

They abide in the *Jade Pure* realm of heaven – on Earth.

They are often born in the first molecule in the womb and stay awake in Tao consciousness while watching as this molecule co-creates sixty-three new fetus molecules.

Worldly Souls

The first kind of soul born in the womb is the worldly soul.

Worldly souls are driven by yin and yang forces.

Attracted to positive or negative movements.

Averting the opposite negative or positive movements.

Constantly counter-balanced by the opposite force.

Bewildered by the four directions.

Never in balance. Never in harmony.

Never seeking the mystic path within.

The Celestial Net Traps the Mind

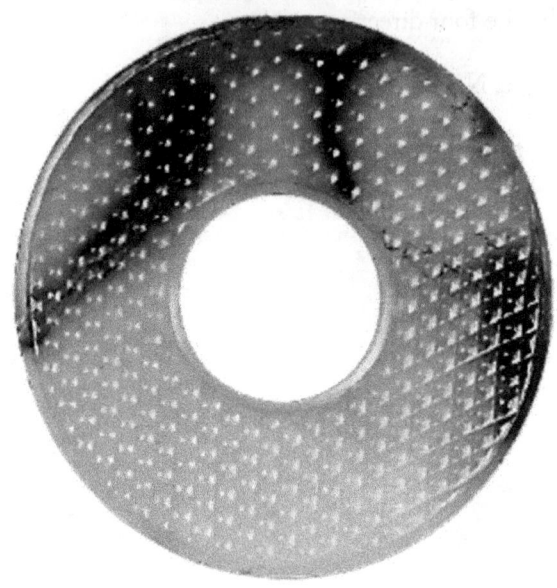

Positive worldly thoughts invite negative thoughts.

Negative worldly thoughts invite positive thoughts.

Positive thoughts push away and hide negative thoughts.

Negative thoughts push away and hide positive thoughts.

Positive thoughts flow into and out of negative thoughts.

Negative thoughts flow into and out of positive thoughts.

Karma knots are created at the intersection of positive and negative thoughts.

Positive emotions invite negative emotions.

Negative emotions invite positive emotions.

Positive emotions push away and hide negative emotions.

Negative emotions push away and hide positive emotions.

Positive emotions flow into and out of negative emotions.

Negative emotions flow into and out of positive emotions.

Karma knots are created at the intersection of positive and negative emotions.

Karmic knots interconnect thoughts and emotions.

Thought and emotions create memories.

Memories of thoughts include the karmic knots.

Memories of emotions include the karmic knots.

Every new thought uses memories of similar thoughts.

Every new emotion uses memories of similar emotions.

All memories are chain-linked to similar memories.

Each new train of thought contacts and compares hundreds of different memories.

Each new train of thought branches out in hundreds of different directions to compare similar memories.

In ignorance, human awareness becomes fragmented

Awareness becomes fragmented with hundreds of thoughts.

Awareness becomes fragmented with hundreds of emotions.

Such a mind is never at rest or at peace.

Such a mind is always active and never restful.

Mind-body awareness creates its own barriers to Tao.

Such a mind is trapped in karmic knots.

Such a mind is trapped in the virtual matrix on Earth.

Such a mind is also trapped in the celestial net in heaven.

New thoughts and emotions create more fragmentation.

You can't experience Tao while trapped in a karmic net.

You can't go within, until you go beyond the net.

You can't see Tao while looking at illusions.

You can't go to heaven while trapped on Earth.

This prison of fragmented mind-body awareness we call

Indra's net, karma, the celestial net, and the virtual matrix.

Getting Lost in Karma

Worldly souls continue moving outward into Maya – during the creation phase of the sojourn of the soul.

They are constantly creating new karma (yin/yang energy patterns).

And reacting to fear and love-based emotions and thoughts.

And have not yet felt the inward pull of Tao consciousness.

They only see themselves doing something.

Worldly souls, thus, become lost in the illusion.

And trapped in an endless web of karma.

Fragmented Awareness

Worldly souls are always searching for stability.

Worldly souls identify with detailed perspectives, opinions and labels:

"I'm a farmer, a politician, a soldier."

"I'm the head of the household."

Because of this, they can never see the totality of it all.

Because of this, they can never be in harmony or balance.

Lacking equipoise, then cannot sense the Tao.

Lost in Personal Perspective

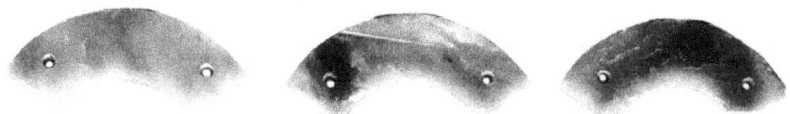

Worldly souls always have a "point of view."

Eventually they identify with detailed personal perspectives

They are always looking outward.

They are always lost in the fragmented patterns of their mind.

They are unaware of the clear awareness within themselves.

Because of this, they can never see the totality of it all.

Because of this, they can never be in harmony or balance.

It can often take one hundred lifetimes as a human to go beyond this stage.

Marked Souls

The second type of soul born in the womb is the marked soul.

After the worldly souls have chased and encountered every desire and fear that can be experienced, and also dreamed every dream that can be dreamed, they reach the turning point in the billion-year journey of their soul.

And then the dissolution phase of the mind begins.

Tired of living in a world of duplicity and misery, and unable to find true happiness in the outside world, they feel a subtle pull within.

Seeking the greater harmony that is starting to form.

Filling the emptiness in their soul with joy and wisdom.

Sometimes, the air begins to glow.

Sometimes, their awareness seems to radiate.

Sometimes, small miracles begin to happen.

Sometimes, their hair begins to rise.

Sometimes, their bodies seem emptier.

Sometimes, their life becomes mysterious.

Sometimes, their path becomes clearer.

Sensing the Clouds and the Winds

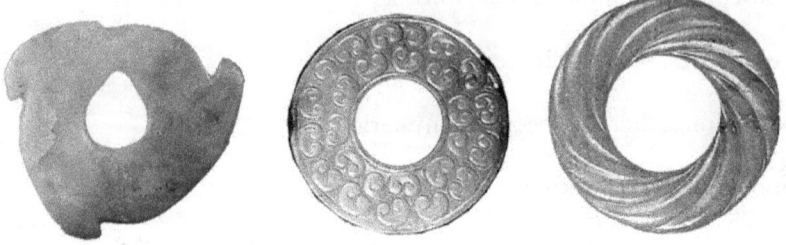

Sensing the presence and the movements of Tao.

Presence = clouds Movement = winds.

Marked souls are old souls – less influenced by yin/yang energies.

And are more attracted to the Ch'ing spiritual energies.

They can often sense the dissolving footprints of the jade sage.

They can often sense the fleeting movements of numinous spirit.

They often search/pray/hope for the yellow dragon to appear.

Flying Through the Celestial Net

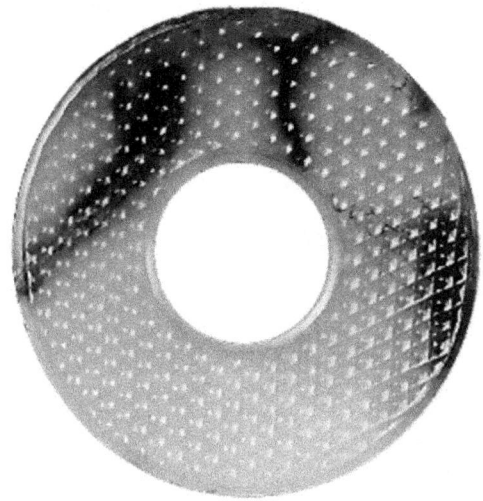

Sensing the divine presence of inward Tao consciousness.

Marked souls turn their attention inward.

Feeling the grace and divinity of Tao consciousness.

Such monks become fully relaxed.

Fully relaxed, such monks instinctively ignore everything else.

Thus, ignoring everything else that comes and goes.

These monks drift away from the pull of the mind.

These monks are easily pulled inward by Tao.

Tao, like a magnet, constantly pulls these monks within.

Fully relaxed these monks melt blissfully within.

Going fully beyond mind-body awareness.

Going fully beyond time-space awareness.

Going beyond all other things that come and go.

Such monks accumulate tremendous grace and merit.

Grace and merit that lasts for lifetimes.

Eventually, in one life or another, a marked soul gains enough merit to easily ignore all mind-body thoughts and emotions.

And such monks thus achieve eye-center enlightenment.

Jade Sage Souls

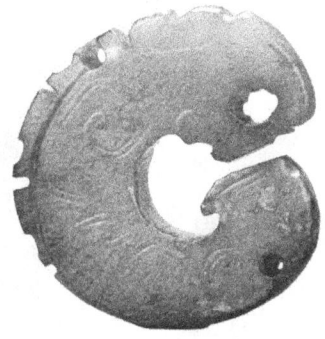 

The third type of soul born in the womb is the yellow dragon.

The yellow dragon, *Yu Shih*, is very often born wide awake.

In the very first molecule of new life in the womb.

Watching their fetus grow from pure consciousness.

In a state of equipoise and *Jade Pure* wu-chi awareness.

Not bothered by PTSD experiences or fears of non-beingness.

In partial remembrance of the complete sojourn of the soul.

Within Wu-Chi Awareness

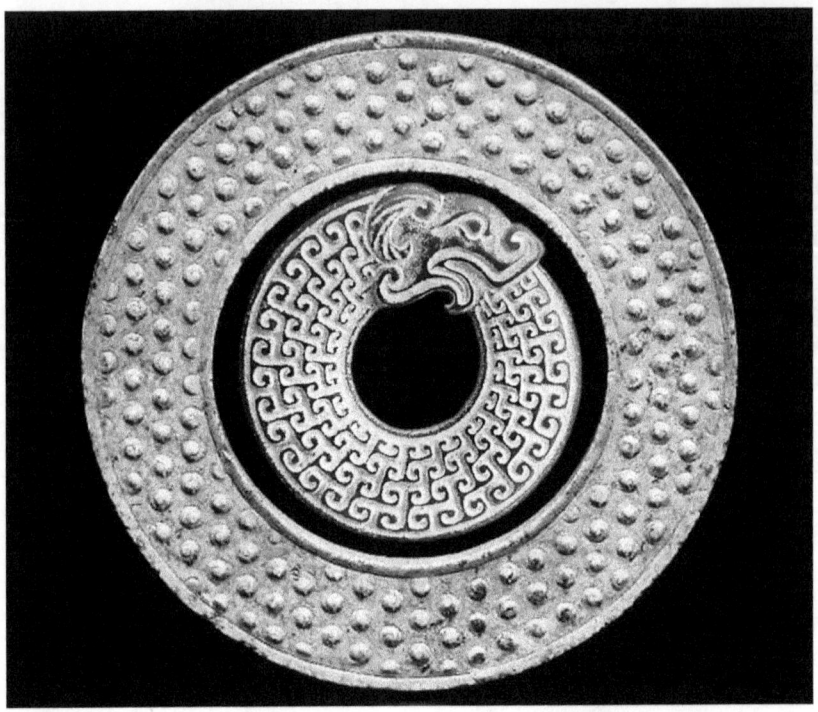

The yellow dragon soul is very rare and leads a very rare life.

There are usually fewer than two yellow dragons on Earth at any time.

Wu-chi awareness is always at the center of their awareness.

And they are always pulled toward complete wu-chi awareness.

Born in a growing state of equipoise and non-blinking focus.

Living a life that is often not even aware of the mind.

Living a life full of small and great miracles.

Their guru/sage is always the *Jade Pure* wu-chi awareness.

The Magical Life of Taoist Monks

Though the monks lead what seems to be an ordinary life.

Filled with yin and yang energies.

And surrounded with an interwoven web of karma.

The old souls look beyond the karma,

And see the arrival of their sage, their inner/outer yellow dragon.

The 3rd Soul Becomes a Jade Sage

The yellow dragon, waiting patiently, hears their call.

The yellow dragon, the Jade sage, knows his/her flock.

They exist within his divine consciousness.

They were within his consciousness when they were born.

He completely understands every potential monk.

And when they are ready, he will appear.

Levels of Tao Enlightenment

Taoist monks feel the inner pull of Tao consciousness.

And eventually melt into Tao consciousness on its way back to heavenly *Jade Pure* Tao consciousness.

Such monks eventually realize and abide in three successive levels, or fields, of Tao enlightenment.

To eventually become Tao Immortals.

3 Levels of Tao Enlightenment

The 3 Stages of Enlightenment for a Jade Sage (Yu Shih)

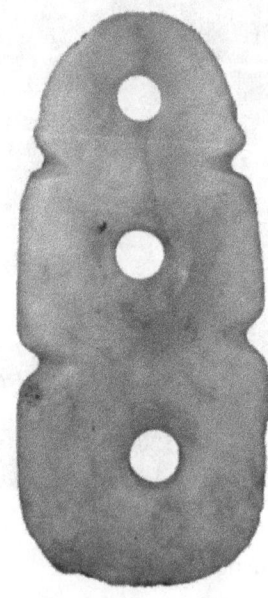

Yu Ch'ing
Heavenly Regions

T'ai-Ch'ing
Crown Chakra

Shang-Ch'ing
Eye Center

Yu-Ch'ing

The *Jade Pure* realm of original Tao.

The realm of Wu-chi Tien-jun.

The lord/emperor of wu-chi.

The complete union with Tao.

T'ai-Ch'ing

The most-pure realm of the crown chakra.

The realm of Ling-pao Tien-jun.

The Lord/Emperor of the precious spirit.

Attaining ling-pao Enlightenment.

Shang-Ch'ing

The high pure realm of the eye center

The realm of Tao-te-jun.

The lord/emperor of virtue, attaining Tao-Te enlightenment.

Jade Sage Is a Yellow Dragon

The jade sage is often called a yellow dragon

The jade sage is like a yellow dragon that looks like a sage on Earth, but is actually a living immortal, the true Yellow Emperor.

The jade sage has wu-chi enlightenment - the highest stage of Tao.

And lives in Yu-Ch'ing - the highest realm of the jade sage.

And lives on Earth to guide disciples back to Tao.

The Jade Sage Is Magical

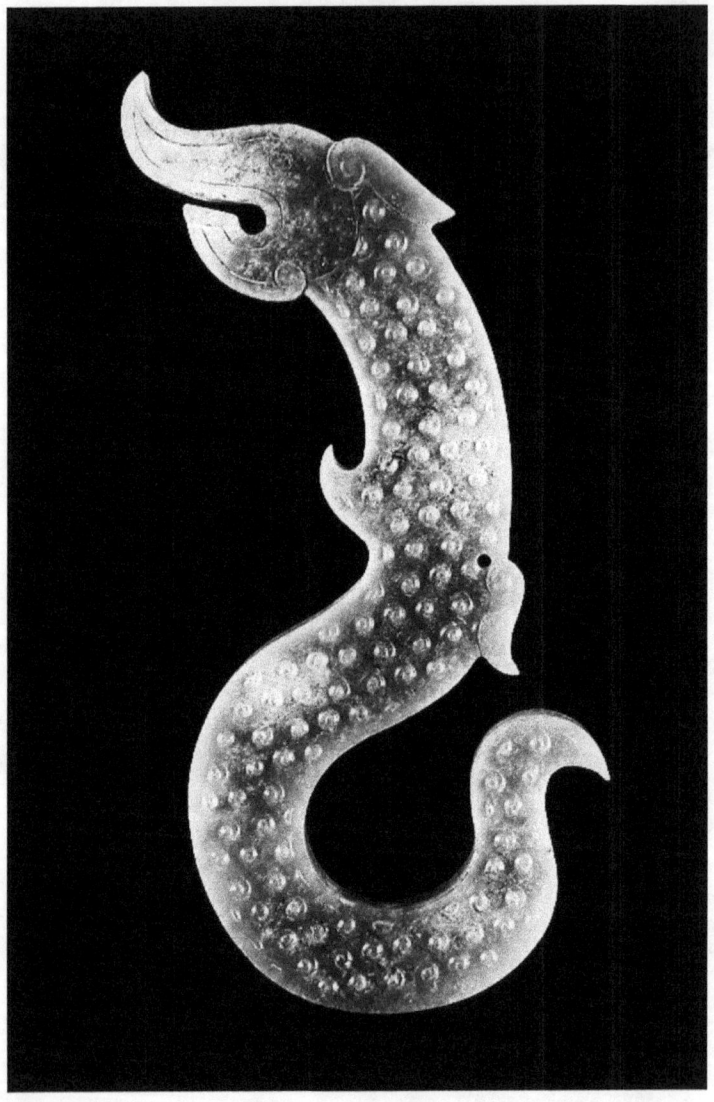

The jade sage is a Taoist saint — filled with magical chi power.

Wherever they walk, miracles automatically happen.

Small, amazing, and great miracles often happen.

They sometimes disappear then reappear later.

The jade sage is immortal —with or without a body.

The jade sage resides in the highest levels of heaven.

The jade sage has *Jade Pure* Tao consciousness.

And lives forever in the highest region of Yu-Ch'ing.

In the highest regions of heavenly awareness.

Abiding eternally in Yu-Ch'ing while on Earth.

Living in a *Jade Pure* consciousness on Earth.

The Three Dragon Gates

Jade Pure Tao consciousness is deep within every monk.

Meditating only on Tao consciousness – which never comes and goes — monks learn to ignore everything else that comes and goes.

Forgetting about thoughts and emotions, they learn to ignore all forms of mind-body awareness.

Holding on the vital essence of Tao consciousness, monks learn to float along with the inward moving streams of Tao.

Floating past the dragon gates of Shang-Ch'ing, T'ai-Ch'ing and Yu-Ch'ing they eventually become *Jade Pure* consciousness.

The Tao-Chih-Tao Mantra

The ancient Chinese Taoist sages taught 2 different mantras to their students. They taught the "Tao-Chih-Tao" Mantra to new students and the "Tao" mantra to advanced students.

First, lets look at the Tao-Chih-Tao mantra.

The Chinese phrase *Tao-Chih-Tao* means *The process of becoming Tao is Tao*.

Tao, like the cultivation of Tao consciousness, is an awakening process. Celestial Tao is continually expanding, like our awareness of Tao as we travel inward.

The Tao-Chih-Tao mantra is most likely the oldest mantra on Earth. It's a mantra that I've repeated thousands of times during previous lifetimes in China. It was also a precious part of the spiritual *download* that I received when I saw my five-thousand-year-old jade tablet in 1995.

The complete sacred mantra is as follows:

Tao-Chih-Tao

Wu-Chih Li Tao

Yu-Chih Li Tao

Tao-Chih Tao means *the process of becoming Tao is Tao*. Generally speaking, people either ignore every form of religion or spiritual path or they outwardly follow a specific religion. The exceptions are those who are pulled within toward and by a spiritual path like Tao consciousness. Tao consciousness, or Celestial Awareness, is ever present at the core of our pure awareness. It acts like a magnet that is always pulling our attention inward. When we simply feel the heavenly/divine presence of Tao, the experience is happening within Tao consciousness.

Wu-Chih Li Tao means *the process of non-beingness benefits all through Tao*. There are three stages of Tao non-beingness: (1) going beyond mind-body awareness — in eye center enlightenment; (2) going beyond awareness of awareness in crown chakra enlightenment; and (3) going beyond all sense of beingness — in the heavenly portal (the Sahaj portal).

Yu-Chih Li Tao means *the process of being benefits all through Tao*. Any Taoist sage who reaches the heavenly regions of *Jade Pure* Celestial Awareness: (1) can create new beings and souls in the creative vortex (*Mother of Tao*); (2) can connect with and nurture/love all beings and other ten thousand things in the heavenly center (*Father of Tao*); and (3) can abide as *Jade Pure* Celestial Awareness in all things and in all beings.

This sacred Tao mantra helps to calm, and then empty, the chaotic mind. Once your mind is empty, your natural awareness becomes more radiant, more blissful, more luminanous, and more harmonically coherent with celestial Tao awareness.

Mystics have always attracted a wide range of students who want to become happier, more spiritually minded, or more divinely attuned.

This mantra is taught to all new students who are still struggling to escape the celestial-net/virtual-matrix of mind-body thoughts and emotions. In the beginning stages of any path, quietly repeating a mantra helps the student to slowly let go of troubling fears and obsessive desires. Worldly students may not be able to easily reach the higher planes of consciousness in a single lifetime, but this mantra will help them to become happier and more productive.

For new students who have felt a divine presence (Tao) in their life, this mantra helps to prepare them for Taoist meditation practices.

The Single-Word "Tao" Mantra

The single-word Tao mantra was taught to advanced monks who were ready, or almost ready, to experience the first stage of eye-center enlightenment.

The ancient single-word *Tao* mantra practice is similar to the modern single word *Om* practice.

The monks were trained to initially practice the tao mantra in the following manner:

- Sitting patiently, calmly, and naturally still,
- Lovingly take three short, relaxed, slow breaths.
- Drawing each deep breath up from the abdomen.
- Following the breath upward in clear awareness.
- Following the breath up into the sinus cavity.
- Pausing to rest in the eye center area.
- Then slowly exhaling,
- With your awareness continuing to rest within the forehead.
- On the fourth breath,
- Compassionately, slowly, and deeply chant the word "Tao" in such a way that:
- The expression of Tao fills the entire breath,
- And causes the breath to vibrate,
- Often causing the breath to become luminous.
- Allow the vibrations to expand outward.
- Allow the energy vibrations to get stronger.
- When the energy begins to collect in your forehead,
- Stay, stay, stay within your forehead.
- Hold on to the clear awareness in your forehead.
- Let your awareness naturally expand.
- Ignore everything else except the clear awareness,
- And the source of your clear awareness.
- The Celestial Awareness that begins at the core of the cosmos flows into your clear awareness.
- Allow your clear awareness to instinctively be aware of the Celestial Tao Awareness flowing into your eye-center bubble/field of awareness.
- Melt, melt, melt away into Tao consciousness.
- Effortlessly float deeper within Tao consciousness.

In this manner, most advanced monks can easily reach eye-center enlightenment.

After achieving and then going beyond eye-center enlightenment, these highly advanced monks can simply point their conscious attention inward to regain the vital essence of Tao consciousness and then melt even deeper into the heavenly regions of Tao consciousness.

Practicing Celestial Tao Consciousness

Tao Is the Middle Way

Ignoring everything that comes and goes enables monks to become silent observers of clear awareness — which never comes and goes.

Abiding in clear awareness enables monks to experience the buzz, the bliss and the beautiful luminosity of Tao in their clear awareness.

Abiding in the buzz and bliss and light of clear awareness enables monks to melt within the single taste of Tao.

The single taste of Tao enables monks to wake up from countless centuries of ignorance and taste the subtle flavors of immortality, and a Tao awareness that seems to be beyond all beyond(s).

Abiding deeply in a single taste of Tao enables new monks to remain in a pristine state of Tao consciousness for many minutes or even hours at time.

Abiding very deeply in a single taste of Tao enables advanced monks to melt into Tao consciousness for many hours or days at a time.

We call this type of monk we a *shifu*.

After learning to abide in the highest regions below the crown-chakra Tao awareness for weeks at a time, a shifu is qualified to teach new seekers about the initial Taoist path to clear Tao awareness.

Disappearing into a single taste of Tao enables enlightened monks to become Tao consciousness for many weeks or months at a time. Such monks are like the legendary yellow dragons who can timelessly travel from Earth and into the heavenly regions of Tao consciousness.

This type of monk we call a *daoshi*.

After learning to abide in the highest regions of *Jade Pure* Tao awareness for months at a time, a daoshi is qualified to teach every aspect of the Taoist Path to Heavenly Consciousness.

After living several lifetimes dedicated to abiding in *Jade Pure* Tao awareness, a daoshi master learns to deeply abide at the source of the cosmos in *Jade Pure* Tao awareness for thousands of Earth years at a time. Later still, such a great sage is able to abide in cosmic *Jade Pure* Tao awareness for millions and then countless trillions of years.

This type of Taoist master is known as *Yuan-shih T'ien-tsun*, the perfect one or *Jade Pure*.

Yuan-shih T'ien-tsun masters have the power of invisibility and are co-creators of the cosmos. The perfect one can see the entire cycle of cosmic creation and dissolution. The *Jade Pure* master arrives like the legendary yellow dragon in the first molecule of the fetus in a perfect state of *Jade Pure* awareness. The perfect one is qualified to teach all new students, all monks, all shifu, teachers and all daoshi masters.

The Differentiated Void

In this divine awareness:

From an individual perspective, you can say that:

There is only the undifferentiated void and the differentiated void.

And that the Tao creates all things.

But Tao awareness is eternal, immortal and timeless,

And Tao awareness is also singular, omnipresent and complete.

There Is Only One Soul, One Tao Consciousness

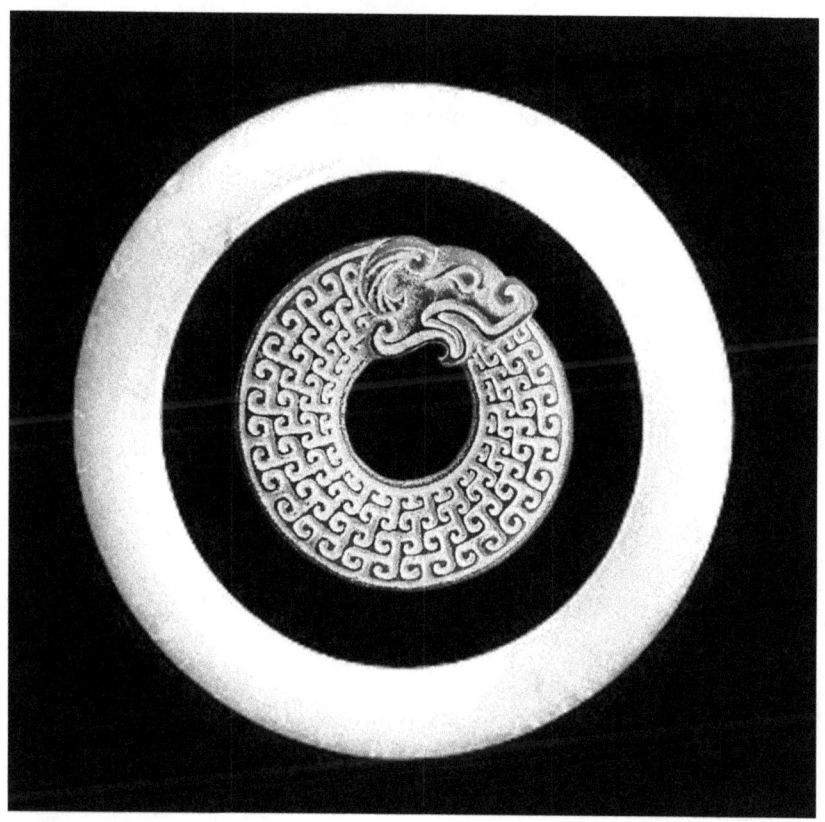

In this eternal awareness:

There is only one soul.

There is only one consciousness.

There is only one true reality.

Tao is every state of human and Tao consciousness.

And within *Jade Pure* Celestial Tao Consciousness,

Celestial Tao is everywhere.

In every object, molecule and point of space.

At the core of everything.

Nurturing, sustaining, and regenerating everything.

As Celestial *Jade Pure* Consciousness.

Ching, Ch'I, and Sheng

To return to Tao:

The soul needs to cultivate waves of conscious Tao energy.

Ching, ch'i and shen waves of conscious Tao energy (aka: Word, Shabd, and Shakti energy).

Through the guidance and love of a jade sage (Yu Shih).

The Taoist path was sometimes called the path of the Jade sage.

As the Middle Way Opens

In the Heavenly presence of Tao, the veil is broken.

As the heaven's currents flow through duality:

Yin and yang powers begin to fade away,

To show the middle way — into equipoise,

The inner way beyond the reach of yin and yang,

The way of the yellow dragon that leads to Tao.

Start Abiding in Equipoise

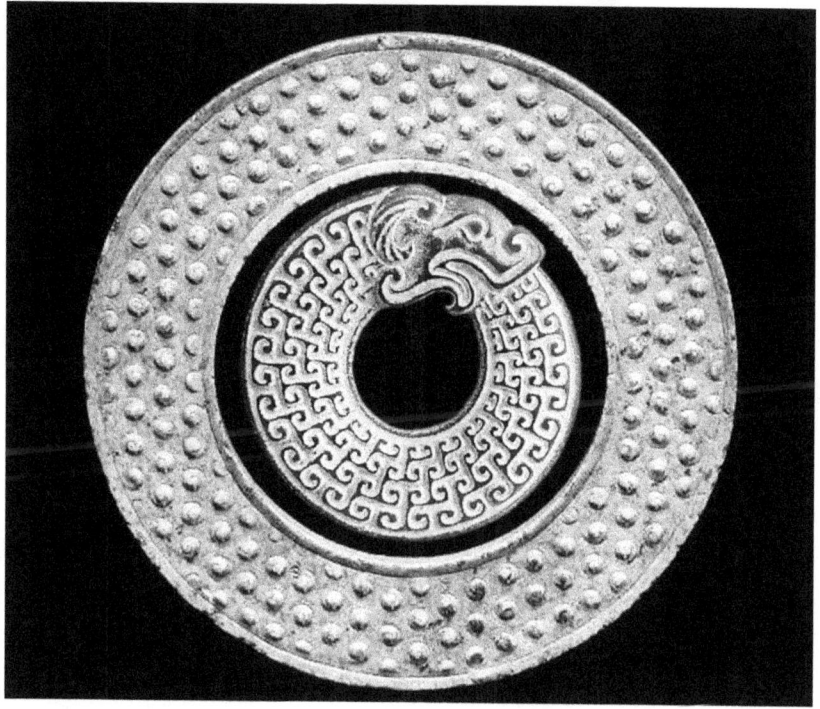

In the middle way, the yellow dragon stays in equipoise,

At the very center of the totality of loving consciousness,

Beyond the reach of yin and yang, of desires and fears,

Beyond the reach of life and death.

Beyond the reach of cosmic creation and dissolution.

Beyond the reach of energy and space.

Beyond all beyond.

Ignore everything that comes and goes.

Ignore the fears that come and go.

Ignore the desires that come and go.

Ignore the physical sensations that come and go.

Ignore the memories and dreams that come and go.

And thus, melt easily into a totality of consciousness.

And thus, easily abide in a blissful, clear awareness.

And thus, expand as your awareness expands.

And thus, float away in Wu Wei clear awareness.

Abiding Inward and Outward

In the middle way, in equipoise:

The emerging sage becomes and emanates harmonic radiance,

Radiating energy, sound currents, light, bliss, and ch'i,

Developing a diamond sharp, non-blinking, focus of attention,

And enough power to evolve rapidly through new layers of consciousness.

Abiding at the nexus point — where the ocean of Tao flows into the drop of human awareness.

Abiding within the River of Tao Consciousness that flows from the heavens, through the monks and then out into the world that all monks live in.

Tao Is Your Inner and Outer Guru

The yellow dragon, Yu-Shih, is *Jade Pure* Tao consciousness.

The jade sage, Yu-Shih, is everywhere within and without.

Yu Shih is always human, the soul, the path and Tao.

Yu Shih will gently lead and pull the soul within.

Yu Shih will tenderly direct and drive the soul forward.

Through the Jade sage the unknown becomes known.

The numinous path becomes radiantly visible.

The four directions clear the way to balance and harmony.

All true monks walk in unison with the jade sage.

True monks float and fly along with and as the jade sage.

True monks melt into the rivers and the winds of Tao.

Yellow dragons support the soul in heaven and on Earth,

Making the wu-wei cultivation of Tao effortless.

Instinctively experience nothing but Tao consciousness.

Instinctively and naturally melt into Tao.

Instinctively and naturally become nothing but Tao.

Let your awareness melt into Tao consciousness.

Effortlessly allow Tao to be everything that you are.

Abide in Joy, Wisdom, and Multiplicity

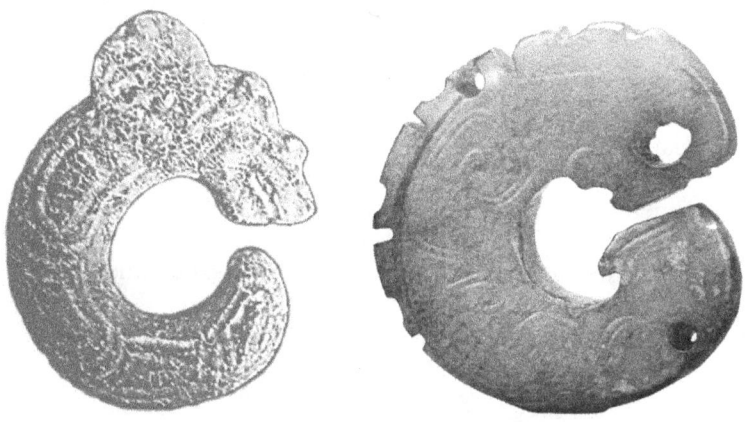

Sometimes the Daoshi master is *like a monkey-dragon*.

Like a great, fun-loving trickster,

Obscuring the path, causing new mysteries and opening new doors,

Causing the disciple to slow down and appreciate the hide- and-seek game between the monks and Tao consciousness,

For the way is not a straight line, and Tao needs to be effortlessly followed — in wonder and awe.

Sometimes the daoshi master is *like a saintly scholar,*

Wise, numinous, mysterious, and yet very simple,

Expounding on the subtleties of the path,

Illuminating the middle way, opening the dragon gate to heaven.

And sometimes the daoshi master is *many different masters,*

Mysteries, wise, quiet, joyful, and serious at the same time,

And expansive, radiant, luminant, and powerful at the same time.

As we move far away from awareness of awareness,

As we get closer to the crown chakra experience,

Of multi-dimensional Tao awareness.

The Path Becomes Easier to Follow

In the beginning, the path is narrow,

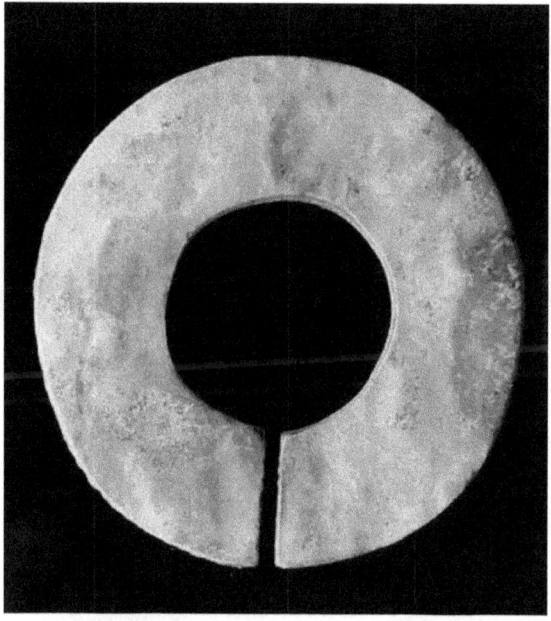

And often shrouded by the mists of the valley spirits.

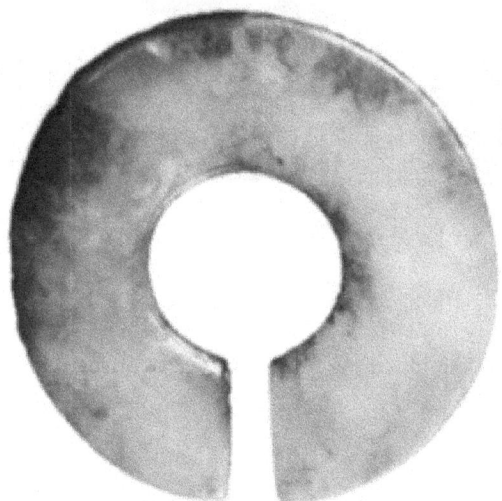

But looking intensely at the path within and without,

Before and beyond the five directions,

In wu-wei harmony and balance,

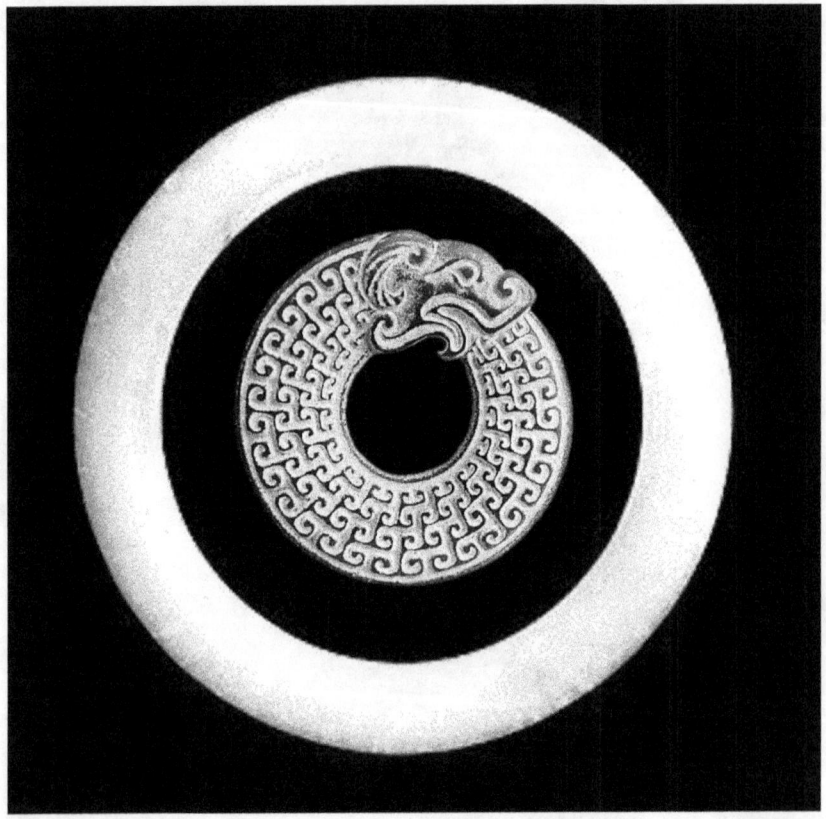

Within the aura of the *Jade Pure* sage,

The numinous path becomes wider and more visible,

Until the path disappears — becoming Tao consciousness.

Tao Consciousness Becomes Everything

And the Tao becomes more real,

Replacing the illusions of the world,

Loosening and destroying the karmic bonds,

Allowing the soul to find his/her own yellow dragon within,

Lifting the monk, in wu-wei, past the eye-center,

Past the crown chakra, where the yellow dragon abides,

And ultimately to full *Jade Pure* enlightenment.

Living within the Magical Middle Way

Worldly Souls, Marked Souls, Jade Sage Souls

The yellow dragon lives mostly within the middle way,

Evolving quickly through the twenty-two levels of human consciousness.

With wu-chi awareness at the center of their awareness,

They often live within bubbles of pure, immersive awareness.

Creating great inventions/books for humankind in their early years,

Then often living a life as a great sage in their later years ,

Or living a life as a great hermit sage in later years.

Becoming the Everlasting Instant

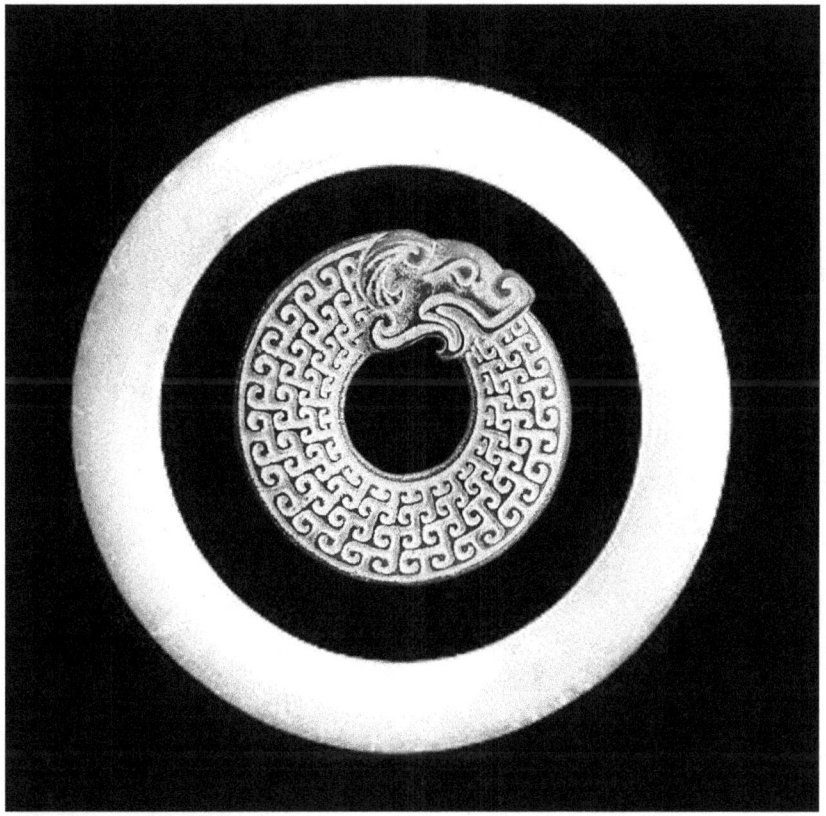

The Tao is a conscious, everlasting instant.

This is the everlasting instant.

An eternal, divine singularity.

At its core it has been called a void, or a zero-field.

It is void of stuff, but it is never void, never empty.

The Tao is a conscious, everlasting instant.

CHAPTER 9

THE TAO OF RAMANA

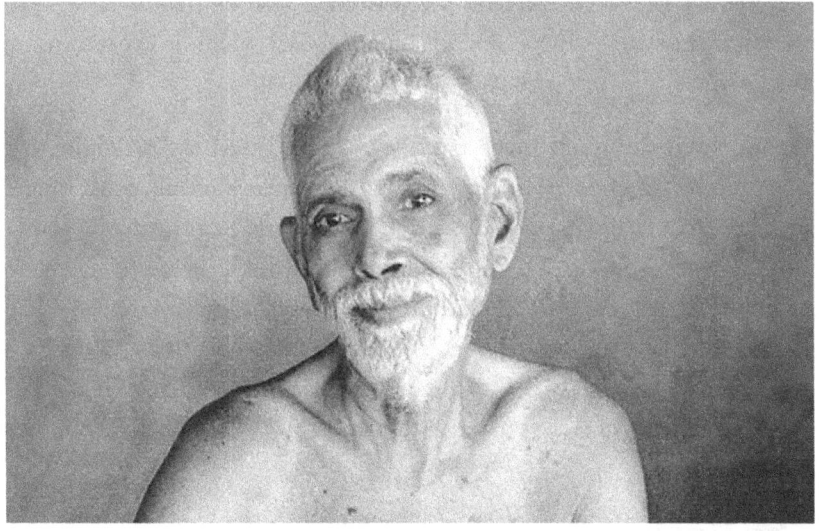

Tao is just a label describing the clear Celestial Awareness that is also at the core of our fragmented mind-body awareness.

Seven thousand years ago, the ancient Taoists taught their monks/students to hold on to Tao during their meditation practices. About one hundred years ago, Sri Ramana taught his jivas/students to meditate with a certainty of sat-chit-ananda. Likewise, for the past ten years,

I've been teaching my mystic friends/students to abide in clear, Celestial Awareness.

These are just different labels and ways that describe the same cultivation method and the same mystical experiences in transpersonal consciousness (beyond mind-body awareness). So let's spend a few minutes comparing the key principles of ancient Tao consciousness to Ramana's consciousness teaching.

The Three Major Levels of Consciousness

About one hundred years ago, Ramana said that when we, as mystics, are no longer attached to, and thus free from the notion that (1) I am the physical mind-body awareness of the eye center, (2) I am the soul's awareness of awareness in the crown chakra, and (3) that I am the causal plane awareness of multidimensional experiences in the heavenly regions, we can then melt into and become the eternal awareness of the pure supreme being (sat-chit-ananda-bliss) which is everything in the universe.

About seven thousand years ago, the ancient Taoist sages taught that once monks are free from the notions that once a monk is no longer attached to (1) having achieved the High Pure Realm of eye center consciousness (Shang-Ch'ing — beyond mind-body awareness), having achieved (2) the Most Pure realm of Crown Chakra awareness (T'ai Ch'ing - beyond awareness of multi-dimensional awareness), and having achieved (3) the *Jade Pure* Realm of Original Tao (Yu-Ch'ing, beyond awareness of Tao awareness), then only celestial Tao awareness will exist.

The Basic Quest

Sri Ramana taught that the real quest is knowing what we are today, to enable us to go back to the origin of where we came from, and what we were at the source of it all.

He reminded his disciples that the inner search for who and what we really are is the only way to remove the resulting evils of our wandering minds. Following this quest to its ultimate origin in supreme awareness is the only way to achieve your natural state of freedom, your natural state of heavenly bliss, and your enlightened state of Celestial Awareness.

The ancient Taoists taught this very same quest – seven thousand years earlier. They taught that in the fragmented awareness of a worldly mind, we know not who or what we really are. The ancient Taoist sages reminded their monks that the inward training path is the ancient path of all yellow dragons and all Taoist saints.

They reminded their followers that they were born to learn how to go beyond the yin and yang dualities of a worldly life, and that they were also born to search for and eventually discover their original nature of heavenly Tao consciousness.

Go Within — Beyond the Mind

About one hundred years ago, Ramana constantly reminded his disciples that the only way to reduce the temptations of the mind to follow the outward energy patterns of thoughts and emotions was to turn your awareness within instead.

The mind, he said, is constantly darting out to follow these trains of thought, and in this process we accidentally, and unfortunately, become the perceiver, the object, and the perception.

He also taught his students that in the interval between two different trains of thought, the light of our inner, greater-self shines brightly. Likewise, he hinted that between all other positive and negative dualities lies the blissful inner path toward supreme awareness. He taught that to know this as the eternal being, and to hold it firmly in your heart, and then to learn to abide in this supreme awareness, one would eventually reach the supreme state of sat-chit-ananda bliss.

Likewise, about seven thousand years ago, the ancient Taoist sages taught that following any trains of thought or emotions creates both attachments to the memories of thoughts and emotions. Eventually such attachments lead to the fragmentation of clear awareness.

But, by holding on to Tao, disciples and monks could float through and beyond all yin and yang states of duality and into Tao consciousness.

These ancient Taoists also taught their monks that by looking inward, they could ignore everything else that comes and goes—like thoughts and emotions.

Looking inward, they would eventually discover a bright, clear awareness that would melt them into a blissful state of Tao consciousness. Then, by simply holding tight to their clear Tao awareness, they could eventually reach the very source of Tao in the heavenly state of *Jade Pure* Tao consciousness.

Going Beyond the Knot of Karma

Maharishi Ramana taught his followers that the illusive, sorrow-laden ego of opposing fears and desires creates karmic knots that bind together the body and the spirit into a lifetime of misery. This mind-body awareness, he said, is the sole cause of every kind of bondage, pain, and sorrow. This mind-body awareness creates the knots that imprison us in a network of false impressions and illusions.

Sri Ramana then went on to discuss the remedy for this illness. The inward practice of self-inquiry he said will gradually sharpen the divine weapon of illuminated, silent awareness, and that with this weapon we can dig out, uproot, and cast away the evil weed of ego. Over time this is the method that will wear away the mind-body knots of ego. It will eventually destroy the delusionary notions that *I am the body*, and *I am the mind*.

Over time, he said that this inward path will result in supreme bliss, heavenly grace, and divine wisdom. Over time it will enable us to achieve supreme awareness.

A long, long, long time ago in ancient China, the Taoist saints were teaching the same lessons. They were teaching their jivas about the miseries caused by the nature of a fragmented mind. They were teaching about the network of misery-laden yin-yang karma that imprisons worldly souls.

And they were also teaching their monks to look within toward the source of their awareness. They taught their monks to search within for the clear awareness of Tao consciousness — that would help to free them from the worldly and the celestial network of mind-body karma. They also taught their disciples that it was often a long and winding road, but one that eventually resulted in the total freedom of their original nature as *Jade Pure* Tao consciousness.

Mantra Repetition Helps New Seekers

Maharaj Ramana taught his new students how to use a simple mantra to steady the mind and to help them to become less emotional. Likewise, he taught his advanced students to spend more time on developing a "certainty of divine awareness."

Sri Ramana often reminded his new seekers that those who cannot easily melt within the silence state of clear awareness to eventually discover the divine source, that inner clear awareness can mentally repeat a mantra — while deeply aware of the divine presence of the greater self. He used to caution his new seekers to meditate with a certainty of sat-chit-ananda-bliss. Ramana taught his disciples that they themselves were the essence of the greater self and through a devoted practice of repeating his mantra they could eventually begin to melt within.

And seven thousand years before Ramana was born the ancient Taoist sages were recommending the *Taoist Tao-Chih-Tao* mantra practice to all new seekers. Advanced monks were instead taught the *Tao* mantra that was aimed at enabling the monks to easily melt into Tao consciousness and to easily remain certain of the inevitability of Tao consciousness. That still holds true today.

Repeating the Tao mantra with devotion will lead to clear awareness far beyond the fragmented awareness of the mind. Repeating the mantra with devotion will lead to a state of Tao consciousness that is beyond all thoughts, emotions, and mind-body awareness.

CHAPTER 10

THE GOLDEN AGE OF TAO

A Time of Chaos

In the twenty-first century, we live in the worst of times for personal survival and in the best of times for the potential of spiritual enlightenment.

We live in a time when disastrous climate changes, crimes against humanity, warfare, corporate greed, oppression, starvation, and worldwide poverty are much worse and significantly more terrifying than they have ever been before.

We also live in a time when greed, spiritual misinformation, and the lack of proper guidance by major religions and would-be gurus are at an all-time high.

We live in a time when the overall chaos, challenges, and lies are often frightening.

Fortunately, we are also living in an era of worldwide spiritual awakening.

Despite the chaos of these troubled times, a new golden age of spirituality enlightenment and Tao consciousness has begun to emerge.

Tired, exhausted, frightened, and often totally disgusted with worldly events, a great and growing number of people from all over the globe are looking inward — instead of outward — for answers, salvation, peace, and spiritual awakening.

As they give up on the empty dreams and hollow promises of the virtual matrix of mind-body awareness, they turn instead to an inward exploration of their soul and the true nature of divine awareness.

The Golden Age Has Begun

Every year, there are more ordinary people having deep spiritual experiences, and even reaching more advanced stages of enlightenment than ever before.

The amazing spiritual stories from near-death survivors are rapidly growing both in numbers and in the depth of spiritual awakening. Millions of teenagers and even children are having lucid dreams and significant, non-cognitive, spiritual experiences.

People from all walks of life, in all religions and from every country on earth, are experiencing a significant increase in precious synchronicities and astounding miracles.

There are hundreds of key spiritual challenges and surprises inside clear awareness.

Unfortunately, most meditation teachers, and students, are simply not aware of how to proceed from the first level of enlightenment to the twenty-second level of celestial enlightenment — way, way, way beyond mind-body and time-space awareness. Most spiritual teachers are also not aware of how to reach multidimensional awareness on a cosmic scale.

But Taoism is a spiritual path of inward training that can be accomplished in a single lifetime with the right teacher, and a strong urge-to-merge into divine enlightenment.

My Area of Focus

There are millions of precious lightworkers on earth right now, and I'm simply one of them.

Lightworkers are old souls who are simply here to serve humankind — through the various psychic and divine skills that they were born with.

There are dozens of different types of lightworkers including various healers, psychics, astrologers, palm readers, mediums, yoga teachers, and meditation teachers. Some teach at a local level, while other lightworkers are using the internet to serve humankind at a much broader level.

Most lightworkers live a simple, modest life that's dedicated to helping others. They are not here to build spiritual empires or to create large bank accounts.

Like most lightworkers, I'm just here to do one thing. I'm here to share my special expertise with the rest of the world or to any other single person who needs my help.

I'm not a guru, a prophet, an avatar, or a priest. I'm not here to create a new religion, a new path, an ashram, a temple, a church, or a loyal following of disciples.

I'm not here to create a lucrative, spiritually minded business, or to become a millionaire by sending out millions of email advertisements a day and charging hundreds of dollars for "dubious" courses to thousands of people every year.

There's way too much misleading information about spirituality and mysticism in the world. There are way too many "popular" gurus and spiritual teachers who simply don't know what they're talking about.

I'm not teaching a dogma that I've learned from some other guru or priest. Nor am I teaching about something that I read in a book. I'm also not teaching a bunch of re-phrased tidbits and nuggets that were scraped together from other websites or books.

It's time to hit the reset button.

I'm only teaching what I've learned from personal experience — which I then cross-validated through the experiences of other mystics.

I'm here to teach what I know extremely well — from more than fifty years of intensive meditation experiences in this life, and in many other previous lifetimes as well. This includes many precious lifetimes in China, South America, Africa, India, and the Mideast.

Like many other simple mystics and teachers, I came into this world as an enlightened soul. But at the same time, I lived an ordinary family life. I worked in factories during high school and college. And I used my spare time to meditate in the deepest levels of Tao consciousness.

And I'm here now to teach Tao consciousness and mystic meditation at significantly new levels of depth and comprehension. And, after I die, there will be additional Taoist sages to explain this path at even greater depths.

Tao consciousness is a bridge to a new level of understanding, including new perspectives about the structure, nature, and purpose of advanced levels of consciousness. It's a bridge between ancient wisdom and modern mysticism. And it's a bridge between the Eastern and Western paths.

Tao consciousness is also a bridge between spiritual mindfulness and the potential to achieve Celestial Awareness in a single lifetime.

Sit back, relax, and be open to the miracles, the clarity, and the bliss that Tao consciousness can produce in your life.

This is what the world needs right now, and the new seekers in the emerging Golden Age of Spirituality will need it even more.

Join us now to learn how to be part of the new Golden Age of Enlightenment.

For more information on Tao:

For more information on the ancient wisdom path of Tao consciousness and on modern Tao meditation practices at the following websites, feel free to join our growing community of Tao Consciousness members at:

www.tao.substack.com
www.gregleveille.com
www.taoconsciousness.com

ACKNOWLEDGMENTS

In so many ways, my life has been a long and winding road of successes and failures, dreams and disappointments. More importantly, it has been a wonderful succession of great friends, teachers, and fellow travelers on the path to Tao consciousness.

To put it simply, I've been very fortunate to have received so much loving attention from so many beautiful people who helped me spiritually and professionally. Without them, I could not have made the spiritual progress that I accomplished. Without these great people, I would not have been able to write this book for you.

First and foremost, I want to thank my loving partner, Conni Mainne, who patiently listened to me as I rambled along and guided me when I needed guidance.

I would also like to thank Eva and Nalle Friedman, Darcia Cowart, Ashley Leveille, Shauna Leveille, Herb and Preeti Verma, Ulla-brit Forsberg, Catherine Halmay, Shirly Martin, Sue Ableidinger, Kee Cheung, Liz Gauthier, Hitesh Tailor, Harjit Sopaul, Rohit Bhardwaj, Pal and Tina Dhillon, David Lee, Sandeep Kataria, Ariadna Pierson, Raj Rajput, Jesse Atwal, Rainer Schmidt, and Sean Waymen for their kind support and friendship.

I am also eternally grateful for the fellowship and wisdom from so many wonderful spiritual teachers including Huai-Chin Nan, Charan Singh, Sharmapa Rinpoche, Karmapa Rinpoche, Sai Maa, Ama, Thich Nhat Hahn, and Captain Ji.

I also want to thank my dear friends and associates at Waterside Productions, who gently and professionally managed the entire production, editing, and marketing of this book. I am also especially grateful to the superb, professional assistance of Josh Freel, my production manager, Jill Kramer, my copy editor, and Joel Chamberlain my interior designer - who individually made this precious book possible. I especially want to thank Bill and Gayle Gladstone at Waterside for their significant assistance and guidance in helping to make this book a reality.

Finally, I want to thank you for reading this book and for your kindness in helping to make this world a more beautiful place to live in.

ABOUT THE AUTHOR

Greg Leveille is a celestially enlightened Taoist sage on a sacred mission to help humankind by reestablishing the ancient path of Tao consciousness. Born in a state of *Jade Pure* Tao consciousness he has been practicing and teaching the beginning and heavenly stages of spiritual Taoist enlightenment and Wu Wei for more than fifty years.

In many ways, Greg has lived an ordinary life as a Boy Scout, a factory worker, a computer programmer, and a high-tech industry executive. But his secret life has been anything but ordinary.

Like a true Taoist sage, Greg's life has been a mystical river of exceptional challenges, near-death experiences, miracles, inventions, and spiritual breakthroughs.

As a young child, new toys would physically manifest and follow him around the house. As a high school student, he was a mathematics prodigy and one of the smartest students in the country.

As a young programmer, he was the original inventor of the first microcomputer operating system, the spreadsheet, and the smartphone.

As an executive, he was widely regarded as the smartest high-tech executive consultant in the world. As a consultant he gave thousands of keynote presentations to the United Nations, the American Medical Association, the International Monetary Fund, multiple countries, and to almost every leading technology company in the computer industry.

For his entire life, he's been dedicated to helping humankind and to creating a mystical bridge between the modern era and the emerging golden age of spiritual enlightenment.

And like most ancient Taoist saints, he patiently waited until his retirement years to begin to publicly teach the path of Tao consciousness. And Greg's new book entitled *Tao Consciousness, before the Tao Te Ching and after Ramana* is a clear indication that the new golden age of spiritual enlightenment has already begun. This is a very magical book with precious how-to advice for spiritually minded seekers at every stage of spiritual enlightenment.

To learn more, visit gregleveille.com.

www.ingramcontent.com/pod-product-compliance
Lightning Source LLC
Chambersburg PA
CBHW071728090426
42738CB00033B/1564